Tales of Old Devon

Other counties in this series include:

Bedfordshire

Buckinghamshire

Cambridgeshire

Cheshire

Cornwall

Devon

Essex

Gloucestershire

Hampshire

Hertfordshire

Kent

Leicestershire

Lincolnshire

Middlesex

Norfolk

Northamptonshire

Nottinghamshire

Oxfordshire

Somerset

Surrey

Sussex

Warwickshire

Wiltshire

Worcestershire

Tales of
Old Devon

~

Sally Norris
With illustrations by Don Osmond

COUNTRYSIDE BOOKS
NEWBURY, BERKSHIRE

First Published 1991
© Sally Norris 1991
Reprinted 2003

COUNTRYSIDE BOOKS
3 Catherine Road
Newbury, Berkshire

To view our complete range of books,
please visit us at
www.countrysidebooks.co.uk

ISBN 1 85306 142 5

Cover designed by Peter Davies, Nautilus Design

Produced through MRM Associates Ltd., Reading
Typeset by Wessex Design & Print Ltd., Warminster
Printed by J. W. Arrowsmith Ltd., Bristol

For Gerry, with love.

Contents

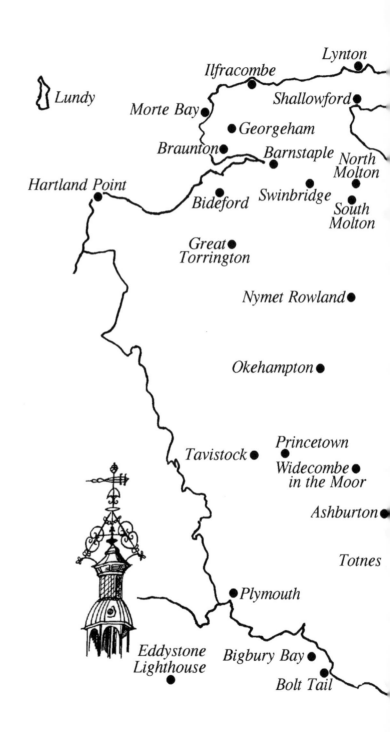

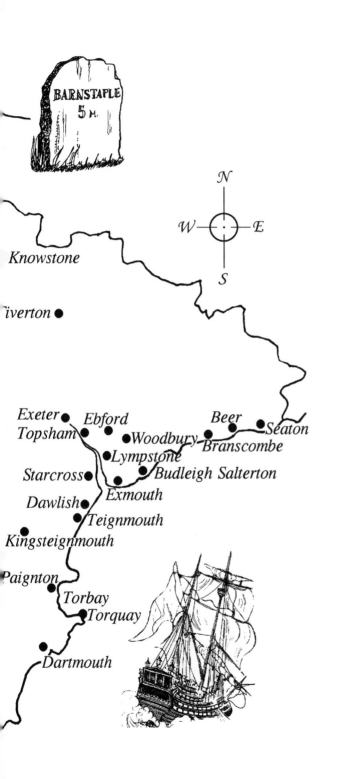

BARNSTAPLE
5 M.

N
W—E
S

Knowstone

Tiverton ●

Exeter ● Ebford   Beer
Topsham ●   ● Seaton
● ● Woodbury ● Branscombe
● Lympstone
Starcross ●   ● Budleigh Salterton
Dawlish ● ● Exmouth
● Teignmouth
Kingsteignmouth

Paignton ●
● Torbay
● Torquay

● Dartmouth

The Smuggler's Tale

TWO hundred years ago, the golden age of smuggling was at its height. Devon's southern coast, lying invitingly close to the French port of Cherbourg and to the Channel Islands of Alderney and Guernsey, was peopled with the hardy and resourceful descendants of sea-rovers, Vikings and naval heroes. It was inevitable that they should become free-traders, smuggling contraband cargo across from the Continent and into the willing hands of their countrymen. They did so in specially-designed boats on an absolutely colossal scale — every year at least one million gallons of French brandy evaded the punitive duties imposed by the British Government, as did about half the tea drunk in England. The Devon smugglers' contribution to this figure was substantial.

Whole communities co-operated in free-trading ventures, and one of the best-known of these was the small, isolated fishing village of Beer, in the south-eastern corner of the county. Its deep, narrow cove, sheltered by tall chalk cliffs honeycombed with caves, proved an ideal spot, and its residents were irresistibly drawn into the smuggling game. One of them became Devon's most famous smuggler — Jack Rattenbury, escapologist extraordinary.

Jack was born in Beer in 1778 and spent his childhood

learning about the harshness of a fisherman's life from his uncle, who believed that frequent beatings were good training for a lad. Anxious for a more swashbuckling, less painful existence, Jack enlisted as a cabin boy on a privateer vessel, the *Dover*, bound for the Azores. He was thrilled at the prospect of the voyage, but after three months of unprofitable inactivity, rations and tempers ran short. Young Jack was beginning to wonder whether anything exciting ever happened on a privateer when the lookout spied a ship worth investigating. The *Dover*'s crew closed up to her, but finding she was flying British colours, prepared to cheer her on. To their consternation, the friendly flag was suddenly hauled down, to be replaced by French colours. The enemy vessel opened fire, and, since she mounted 26 guns, the *Dover*'s captain promptly surrendered.

The whole crew was transferred to the French privateer and taken to Bordeaux, where they were imprisoned. Fourteen year old Jack, having charmed the French sentries with his boyish friendliness, wormed a forged pass from one and so pulled off the first of the many escapes which punctuated his career. His return to England, however, was not quite as straightforward as he had hoped. He found sanctuary on an American boat in harbour, only to discover that she was not allowed to leave because of the French embargo on foreign shipping. He was forced to kick his heels on board for a year, before the vessel was finally granted permission to sail for New York. Here, Jack found a berth as cook and cabin boy on a brig departing for Le Havre. Having twice crossed the Atlantic safely, he thought the last stage of his long voyage, just a trip across the English Channel, would be soon over. Not a bit of it! Severe gales blew them off course as far as Norway, where they remained for three months, sheltering from atrocious storms.

When Jack at last set foot again in Beer, he was a very different lad to the green youngster who had blithely set forth in search of adventure almost two years before. Of course, he was overjoyed to see his mother and to tell vivid stories of his exploits to his friends, but he was soon bored by the dull routine of catching fish for a living. He wanted more from life than that. The smugglers of Beer beckoned to him; joyfully, he joined them.

They made a number of trips to Alderney, the closest of the Channel Islands. Here, at a port exempt from customs duty, and just a short hop from the French coast, they could fill their lugger with kegs of brandy, rum or gin, topping up the cargo with whatever else was available — tea, tobacco, silk, lace, salt — a huge variety of luxury goods which, under ordinary circumstances, were quite beyond the means of common folk. The free-traders could make a good profit and still sell the goods well below the official price. Jack greatly enjoyed his first taste of smuggling and made a little money, but at the end of four months the lugger was laid up for repairs. Needing a job, he signed on with a freighter bound for the coalfields of South Wales.

Once again his voyage was cut short by the unwelcome attentions of a French privateer. The English seamen were removed from their ship, but Jack was left behind with a French boarding party of five, who were to take their prize across the Channel. Fortunately, they proved more interested in drinking and carousing below decks than steering the ship, and he was left alone with instructions to make for the nearest French port. Thick fog descended, blotting out landmarks, but allowing Jack, already an expert navigator in his home waters, gradually to head for the Dorset coast. When the befuddled prize-master emerged, demanding to know their position, Jack convinced him they were nearing Cherbourg, although they were actually approaching Swanage! English voices hailing them from a small boat alerted the Frenchman to the sad error he had made in trusting the Devon lad. Jack decided the time had come to bid his companions 'adieu' and leapt overboard, accompanied by a string of oaths and bullets. Having struggled ashore, he was desperate that the enemy did not get away with their prize. He found Captain Robert Willis of the naval cutter *Nancy* and breathlessly told his tale. The intrepid captain set off in pursuit and recaptured the English brig without much difficulty. Jack hoped that the ship's owners would reward him for his quickwittedness, but he was disappointed — not a penny piece came his way.

Whenever he could, he continued to join in smuggling runs. Many of these were successful, but there were inevitable setbacks when the Revenue men were on his tail and the contraband had to be hastily dumped overboard with the fervent hope that it could be recovered later. This evasive action was called 'sowing the crop'; the brandy tubs, half-ankers holding between four and five gallons, were strung together, weighted with stones and sunk. When it was safe, the 'crop' could be retrieved by using grapnels, called 'creepers'. Sometimes the Revenue men found the 'crop' first and seized it; sometimes a spell of bad weather meant that they lost the markers and thus the whole cargo. Jack had plenty of thrilling times, but could not seem to make as much money as he had anticipated.

In the spring of 1806, he was returning from Alderney on a lugger laden with brandy tubs when he was intercepted by the Revenue cutter *Duke of York*. The smugglers sank as much as they could, but a few tubs were still floating on the surface when the cutter reached them, and these were quickly seized. The captain promised Jack that he would let them all go free with their boat if they would just recover the jettisoned cargo for him. They did as he asked, but then found that he had no intention of keeping his word. They were all arrested and taken to Dartmouth, where they were tried in front of a magistrate. The usual choice of punishments were offered to the smugglers — £100 fine, a spell in gaol or a stint in His Majesty's Navy. They all opted for prison, but after a few hours confined to a stinking dungeon decided that the

Royal Navy was the lesser of the evils. Jack, however, stayed less than 24 hours on his new ship before diving overboard and scuttling home.

Soon after this unpleasant experience, Jack had another. Returning from Alderney in a rowing boat weighed down with yet more brandy, he and his mates were overhauled by the sloop *Humber*, commanded by Captain Hill, and arrested. This time, not even Jack's creative brain could dream up an escape plan. They were tried at Falmouth and sent off to Bodmin Gaol under heavy guard. But the constables made frequent stops on the journey for refreshment, and by the time they reached Indian Queens, were becoming quite merry. Our resourceful smuggler grabbed his opportunity, slipped his bonds and disappeared before they knew what was happening. Two days later, he was home again. He decided to lie low for a while.

Sooner or later, of course, he was bound to be caught and confined. Another brush with a patrol vessel landed him in Exeter Gaol for six months. This did not deter him from returning to smuggling immediately he was released — he was in desperate financial trouble and, with his wife Anna and four children depending on him, needed money urgently. He was arrested again off Dawlish in December 1825 by members of the newly-formed Coastguard service — an increasingly efficient body. He spent a miserable Christmas in the lock-up at Budleigh Salterton before being sentenced to 15 months in Exeter Gaol.

He was released in April 1827, and in June was in London. In an extraordinary tribute to his excellence as a mariner and pilot, he was selected by the local VIP, Lord Rolle, to give evidence before Parliamentary committees in the Commons and the Lords concerning the construction of a harbour at Beer. His intimate knowledge of the coast impressed all his eminent questioners. He went home, well pleased with his performance and with the guineas given to him by Lord Rolle. Within a fortnight he had been smuggling again, was chased by the cutter *Invincible*, sank his kegs and lost the lot.

In November 1831, he and his crew were caught in Seaton Bay, tried at Lyme, fined £100 and sent to Dorchester Gaol for 14 months. By the time he was free, in 1833, Jack was considering retirement. One or two more trips, with the Coastguard men always on the look-out, persuaded him that enough was enough. His smuggling days were over.

Jack Rattenbury remains a famous smuggler, when the names of most of the others have long been forgotten, because a book of his memoirs was published in 1837, seven years before his death. This unrivalled document was written, not by the man himself, but by a discharged Unitarian minister from nearby Seaton, the Rev John B. Smith. A more unlikely collaboration can hardly be imagined, the man of God listening enthralled to Jack's colourful tales, perusing his sketchy journals and then rendering them into a wonderfully readable chronicle of a smuggler's life and adventures. Even odder, the pair were introduced at Shute House by Sir William Pole, Deputy Lieutenant of Devon, who suggested the idea of a book. Smith, grindingly poor and on the verge of starvation, was glad to undertake the task. The result is an amazingly full account of Jack's ups and downs in which his irrepressible humour, faithfully translated by John Smith's pen, comes shining through on every page.

> 'Thus ended my career as a smuggler — a career which, however it may be calculated to gratify a hardy and enterprising spirit, and to call forth all the latent energies of the soul, is fraught with difficulty and danger; in following which, many and various have been the expedients to which I have had recourse, in order to escape detection, baffle pursuit, and elude the vigilance of those indefatigable picaroons which every where line our coasts.'

Tarka Country

F OR many of us *Tarka the Otter* is one of childhood's
happiest memories. Tarka's lovable personality,
exciting adventures and dreadful death can still seem vivid
several decades later. But something we perhaps
remember less clearly is where exactly the tale takes place.
So it may come as a surprise to discover that Tarka's travels
— all in Devon — can be precisely located. As the
introduction to the Puffin edition of Henry Williamson's
novel says, 'With a good map you can follow almost every
step of the story, every twist and turn of the rivers.' Indeed,
tracing Tarka's tracks has become so popular that his part
of Devon is now called Tarka Country.

Nobody knew the area better than Williamson himself,
even though he was not born a Westcountryman and did
not arrive in Devon, in 1921, until he was 25. By then he
was already haggard and grey-haired, shattered by four
unspeakable years in the trenches of Northern France.
When the war ended, he tried to earn a living in Fleet
Street, but could not adjust to the petty irrelevancies of
peacetime existence. Shell-shocked and irritable, he
quarrelled with his father and was thrown out of the house.
He jumped on his 499cc BRS Norton and headed for
Devon, where he felt drawn because of his mother's family
connections. He reached the small town of Georgeham,
seven miles from Barnstaple, just above Braunton
Burrows, and looked for somewhere to live. He found
Skirr Cottage — rent one shilling and sixpence a week —
and moved in with the resident family of barn owls
comfortably nesting under the thatch. Delighted by their

company, Williamson painted an owl in white and gold above the doorway, thereafter using that bird as a symbol for the title page and end page of his books. He was also joined, at ground level, by a dog and cat.

Sometime later he rescued an otter cub whose mother had been shot by a farmer. He took him home and tried to make him drink some milk, though without success. Since the cat had just had a kitten, he put the tiny thing in with her, but she rejected him. He then had the idea of rubbing the cub's face and body against the kitten. Next time he tucked the cub in with the mother cat she accepted him without surprise and reared him with her kitten.

The little otter prospered and was soon able to eat from a saucer. He had fun in the bath when water was squirted on him and followed Williamson everywhere, playing in the streams around Georgeham. But on one of their walks he suddenly screamed in agony. His paw had been caught in a rabbit trap. Williamson managed to prise him from the serrated steel spring, though at the cost of three of the otter's toes. As he was wrapping him in his coat to take him home, the poor frightened creature squirmed from his grasp, jumped to the ground and ran away. Williamson looked everywhere until night fell. He spent all next day hunting for him, hoping at least to come across a print of his maimed paw. But he found nothing. The weeks passed, and he widened his searches, going south to the Taw-Torridge estuary and then up both the Taw and Torridge nearly to their sources, seeking him in otter haunts as far away as Okehampton. After several months he abandoned his quest. But during that time the story of Tarka (Old Celtic: 'little water wanderer') was born, and in writing it Williamson was once more united with his lost friend.

Because Tarka's life was so real to Henry Williamson, it is hardly surprising that he set the story in a real place, the corner of North Devon where he searched for his lost otter. Tarka was born at Owlery Holt on the Torridge — 'he was less than five inches long from his nose to where his wee tail joined his backbone. His fur was soft and grey as the buds of the willow before they open at Eastertide.' Owlery Holt is just north of Canal Bridge, between Great Torrington and Weare Giffard; the old oak tree there among whose roots Tarka spent his earliest days is gone, but 13 saplings have been planted in its place. Canal Bridge is where Williamson is said to have dreamt up the idea of *Tarka the Otter* while leaning on the parapet and gazing at the river. The disused railway line nearby has been converted into a footpath and provides wonderful views of much of the area where Tarka frolicked in his cubhood.

The twelve-mile stretch of the Torridge between Huish and Bideford is the setting for the first six chapters of the book and for the last four, making it the heart of Tarka Country. Here, Tarka was born and died, and in this area his father, sister and son were also killed. His beloved White-tip gave birth to their four cubs in a holt on the river Duntz, a tributary of the Torridge, west of Weare Giffard.

One of the best known places associated with Tarka is Town Mills (now called Orford Lodge), on the outskirts of Great Torrington, where he briefly shook off his pursuers by hiding in the stationary millwheel during the workmen's lunch hour. 'He drew himself on to the hatch and walked slowly up the wet and slippery wooden troughs to the top of the wheel. He squatted low and watched the grating. Hounds swam along it and Deadlock pushed his black head in the space of the missing bar.' When the workmen returned and lifted the hatch, 'the wheel shuddered and moved. Water gushed in and over each trough as it was lowered on the rim, and the wheel began its heavy splashing trundle. Tarka was borne down into darkness and flung on the rock.' The wheel still turns there years later and is an ideal spot from which to begin a Tarka ramble.

Apart from going up and down the Torridge and Taw, including onto Dartmoor, Tarka travelled to the north coast of Devon and west from Lynton to Ilfracombe, round Morte Point and down to the Taw-Torridge estuary. During an earlier foray at Braunton, he was caught in a trap and saved by his first consort, Greymuzzle, who freed him by biting off three of his toes, then lost her life while defending him from a farmer's collie.

Williamson obviously derived pleasure from having Tarka pass by Skirr Cottage on his second visit to the Georgeham area. 'The stream flowed below a churchyard wall and by a thatched cottage, where a man, a dog, and a cat were sitting before a fire of elm brands on the open hearth. The wind blew the scent of the otter under the door, and the cat fumed and growled, standing with fluffed back and twitching tail beside her basket of kittens. . . . The cottage door was pulled open, the spaniel rushed out barking. A white owl lifted itself off the lopped bough of one of the churchyard elms, crying *skirr-rr*.'

Most of *Tarka* was planned at Skirr Cottage and finished in 1927 at the author's new, equally modest home, now known as Crowberry Cottage, a few doors away. By then he was a married man with a small son, Windles, the first of his six children. His wife and child were in poor health, so he had to look after them, the house and animals and still try to fit in his novel, which he tackled at night, often while cradling the fretful babe in his left arm. When *Tarka* was published, it drew golden opinions from Thomas Hardy and John Galsworthy. It also won the Hawthornden Prize. Williamson's financial situation improved, and his writing also flourished. Over the next 50 years, until his death in August 1977, he produced another 45 titles, including *Salar the Salmon* (1935) and a huge 15 volume semi-autobiographical saga *A Chronicle of Ancient Sunlight* (1951–1969).

After the success of *Tarka* he moved to Shallowford, a village between Swimbridge and South Molton. In 1937 he bought on impulse a dilapidated 240 acre Norfolk farm that cost him little at the time but destroyed his marriage

20

and spurred Windles into punching him in the face and emigrating to Canada. Another setback was internment in the local jail because of his openly proclaimed admiration for Hitler, though he was soon released as a 'harmless eccentric'.

By the end of the war he had transformed the farm into a Grade A establishment. He returned to Georgeham, minus his wife and all six children, and remarried, but his second wife left him too. He had always been both crotchety and charming, a wayward spirit who outraged pompous folk and amused ordinary ones — dancing the can-can on a pub table when in his seventies — but he gradually became less of a charmer and something of a misanthrope. He died a lonely man, cared for at the last by the monks of Twyford Abbey. He is buried in the same Georgeham churchyard that Tarka ran past. The elmboard writing hut overlooking the sea, which he built in a nearby field, still stands. Many of his possessions have been faithfully preserved there by the Henry Williamson Society, and on the walls are the faded terrifying First World War photographs that he pinned up as a permanent reminder to himself of the horror he had experienced.

Tarka the Otter swims joyfully on, loved all over the world in many languages — the Russians buy a hundred thousand copies a year. Now this little otter has inspired Devon County Council's Tarka Project, which uses his story as a theme for protecting and enriching the wildlife, natural beauty and special character of North Devon, encouraging interest in the area and promoting conservation, recreation and tourism. Tarka Country is bounded by a fascinating 180 mile pathway, the Tarka Trail, enclosing the wedge-shaped tract of land from Okehampton to the north coast. It was opened in 1991, and in 2002 the centre of Tarka Country, around the Taw–Torridge estuary, was designated the first UNESCO biosphere reserve in the UK.

*THE FIRST
EDDYSTONE
LIGHTHOUSE
1698*

The
Eddystone
Light

SINCE 22nd July 1981 the most famous lighthouse in
Britain, 14 miles south-west of Plymouth, has been
without a keeper. Man has been replaced by machine.
Silently, inevitably, Eddystone's 570,000-candlepower
beam flashes twice every ten seconds, visible for 28 miles.
When banks of fog obscure the brilliant light, the mournful
blasts of its six foghorns sound three times a minute,
warning shipping up to five miles away of the treacherous
Eddystone Reef. But behind this seemingly effortless
automation lie three centuries of extraordinary
endeavour, excitement and disaster.

The Reef had claimed countless ships and lives before
work began on the first lighthouse in 1696. This
pagoda-like structure was designed by Henry Winstanley,
a highly gifted inventor rather than trained architect. He
was also a successful merchant and showman —
'Winstanley's Water Theatre', near Hyde Park, drew large
crowds for years. He was imbued with immense
self-confidence, with no qualms about making the first
attempt to build a lighthouse on a rocky ledge in the open
sea. He had patience and endurance, too, because for six
months at the start he and his team rowed across from
Plymouth each day, spending the few hours available at low

water struggling to gouge twelve deep holes in the almost impenetrable granite. Their pickaxes and sledge-hammers blunted or broke on the unyielding rock. Waves swirled round their feet, making the surface slippery; tools often flew from their grasp when the handles became wet. Eventually twelve iron shafts were sunk and secured in the holes, and the building began to rise above sea level.

By June of the following year construction was proceeding well when a French privateering frigate dropped anchor near the Reef and sent over a rowing boat loaded with corsairs who took Winstanley prisoner! Without further ado he was hustled aboard the frigate which immediately set sail for St Malo. As England and France were at war, our hero was minutely questioned about his activities on the Reef. Louis XIV got to hear about his English captive's efforts to build a lighthouse, and summoned him to Versailles. Recognizing the importance of his work to all mariners, the Sun King released Winstanley straight away, and sent him safely home, weighed down with gifts.

The lighthouse continued to grow, finally reaching a height of 80 ft, surmounted by an ornate weathervane. On Monday 14th November 1698, after two and a half years' toil, Winstanley climbed into the lantern and lit the tallow candles, which are thought to have been visible at a distance of three or four miles. Ships arriving at Plymouth brought the amazing news that Eddystone was now in operation; the lighthouse was acclaimed as one of the wonders of the modern world. Winstanley, however, was prevented from viewing his creation or receiving the public's congratulations for another five weeks, because continuously rough seas made it impossible for any vessel to reach him. He and his men were not taken off until three days before Christmas, when they were close to starvation. With his usual ingenuity Winstanley had devised conjuring tricks to help keep up their spirits.

The first lighthouse keeper and his family moved in at

once. They had to plan their days carefully, since the candles needed replacing every three hours. When Winstanley visited them early in the spring he found everything running satisfactorily, but was alarmed to notice that some cement pointing of the stonework at the base of the tower was rapidly eroding, undermined by the ceaseless watery bombardment. The keeper said that sometimes the waves were so huge that they swept right over the lantern, 60 ft above the Reef. Winstanley decided the building must be strengthened. He made the walls much thicker and increased the height by 40 ft, completing these alterations in autumn 1699. The lighthouse now presented a picturesque image with verandah, balustrade and projecting bow window. It also boasted pious inscriptions such as *Glory Be to God.*

Winstanley was now so certain of his creation's stability that he frequently spoke of hoping he could be in the lighthouse during 'the greatest storm that ever was'. His wish came true. On the morning of Friday 26th November 1703 he put out from the Barbican with some workers to effect a number of repairs. Men on the quay warned him that the weather seemed to be deteriorating, but he said he welcomed the chance of defying the elements from the security of his island fortress. That night, the worst storm recorded in English history rampaged across the country, destroying thousands of buildings, including 400 windmills and 100 churches. Surveying the wreckage of their homes, many sleepless, terrified people assumed that Judgement Day had arrived.

In the West Country, salt from the sea was blown 25 miles inland; rivers burst their banks. The Severn rose eight ft higher than ever known, drowning 15,000 sheep. Among the hundreds of fatalities were Bishop Richard Kidder and his wife who were buried beneath tons of masonry at Wells. In Plymouth the devastation was worse than anywhere else, stretches of the city completely flattened, the foreshore piled with debris. So much shipping was lost in the South West that for a short period, without his realizing it, Louis XIV had England at his mercy.

On the day after the Great Storm a boat went to the Eddystone Reef, but nothing of the lighthouse remained. Henry Winstanley, aged 59, his workers, the keeper and his family, had all been swept away. Elizabeth Winstanley, his widow, petitioned that he was owed a substantial amount of the £5,000 he had spent on the building, which was commissioned by the Corporation of Trinity House in London. She was granted a pension of £100 a year.

Within days of the catastrophe a merchantman from Virginia, the *Winchelsea*, went to pieces on the Reef and was followed by a succession of other unfortunate vessels. It became imperative to erect a second Eddystone Light. This time the architect, John Rudyerd, was a silk mercer! The son of a Cornish labourer, he owned a shop on Ludgate Hill in London. Why he was chosen to design the lighthouse remains a puzzle, but the building he produced was highly effective. Unlike Winstanley's, it was completely round with an absence of projecting bits and pieces that made it more suitable for withstanding the heavy seas. The structure consisted mostly of oak timbers bolted and clamped together, the base filled in solid with stone. Once again all the materials had to be transported from Plymouth to the Reef in barges. In spite of the difficulties of working on the Reef, Rudyerd's men erected the lighthouse in only three years. The lantern was lit on 28th July 1708 and the building finished shortly afterwards. The cost was £10,000.

This second lighthouse defied the elements for nearly 50 years, until on the night of 2nd December 1755 the top of the lantern caught fire. The keepers tried to extinguish the blaze with buckets of water, but the flames crept down the tower, driving the three men from floor to floor and eventually out onto the rocks. Fortunately, they were rescued by fishermen who threw ropes to them and dragged them through the waves to safety. The lighthouse burned for five days and was totally destroyed.

One of the keepers, Henry Hall, aged 94, complained of severe stomach pains. He said that while he was hurling water up into the flames, molten lead from the roof poured into his open mouth. Nobody believed him. He died twelve days later, and a post mortem by Doctor Spry of Plymouth revealed a half-pound lump of lead in his abdomen! Doctor Spry's amazing discovery was doubted by learned colleagues, who insisted that a man could not possibly survive twelve days with a stomach full of lead. This so infuriated the surgeon that, to prove his point, he experimented on animals, pouring lead down their throats and noting how long it took them to die.

During the period when the next lighthouse was being planned and built, Trinity House moored a lightship beside the Reef, but the vessel could not keep to her anchorage. On eight occasions she broke away altogether and drifted several miles off, proving to be a fatal hazard to ships which assumed she was marking the Reef.

The third lighthouse, designed by John Smeaton, was similar to Rudyerd's but made of stone. Local granite was used for the foundations and facing; the overall weight was nearly 1,000 tons. Smeaton, a clockmaker by trade, invented a number of ingenious·devices to save precious time on the Reef, such as quick-drying cement and a hoist for lifting blocks of stone. Even so, the new Eddystone took three years to build. Many of his workers were tough Cornish tin miners — just the sort of men that the Navy press-gangs were looking for. In order to stop having his employees filched from under his nose, Smeaton arranged with the Admiralty to have a medal struck for each man, which was worn to prove he was working on the lighthouse.

But the weather remained the chief enemy. One afternoon in November 1756 he and his team left the Reef for Plymouth and, finding the sea running too strongly against them, altered course for Fowey. They could not make that port and were driven down past Mevagissey, Falmouth, the Lizard and out into the Channel towards the Bay of Biscay. It took four days of back-breaking effort to sail and row their way home, by which time, without food or water, they were on the point of collapse.

Smeaton's light — 24 tallow candles — sent its first beams across the water on 16th October 1759. It could be seen six miles away. The lighthouse was tended by three men, whose annual salary was £25. Smeaton, writing in 1791 about the building of the Eddystone, seemed rather amused by the popularity of the light-keeper's post.

'To elderly seamen it may be considered as an asylum something like equivalent to Greenwich Hospital . . . John Ireland is the senior of the present set . . . I found him there in the year 1766, in the year 1777, and in my last visit in 1787.'

One of the keepers was so attached to his tower that he refused shore leave for two years. When he was eventually persuaded to go, he went straight to an alehouse and got drunk. He remained completely sozzled during his entire holiday and was returned to the lighthouse still intoxicated. Unfortunately, the shock to his system was so great that he could not recover his senses, and he died on the Eddystone a couple of days later. He would have been proud to know that his lighthouse was so solidly built that it lasted for 120 years before the rocks beneath gave signs of instability.

The present lighthouse, erected on another part of the Reef and weighing 4,500 tons, was designed by Sir James Douglass and finished on 18th May 1882, costing £60,000. For more than a year the two buildings stood side by side; there exists a remarkable painting by R. B. Beechey showing them together like giant chess pieces. Smeaton's lighthouse was then carefully dismantled and re-assembled on the Hoe at Plymouth, where it soon became one of the city's most striking tourist attractions. Thousands visit it every year, climbing the 93 steps of the ever-narrowing spiral staircase, then up wooden ladders to the gallery at the top. The view of Plymouth is breathtaking, and on a clear day you can just see the outline of the present lighthouse.

If you have not been to Smeaton's lighthouse, you should go at the next opportunity. But mind your head when you negotiate the stairs — people were rather shorter in 1759! Of course, the lighthouse may already be familiar to you without your realizing. It was next to Britannia on the old penny coin withdrawn in 1970.

The Dancer and the Frog-Prince

IN France during the summer of 1909 Isadora Duncan and Paris Singer became lovers. Isadora, aged 32, was the great American dancer whose revolutionary approach to her art would profoundly influence modern ballet. Paris, 42, had inherited the millions of dollars which his father, Isaac Singer, earned by inventing and manufacturing the first domestic sewing machine.

In May 1910 Isadora gave birth to their son Patrick at Beaulieu, near Nice. This prompted Paris to suggest they should marry, but Isadora pooh-poohed the idea. 'How stupid for an artist to be married!' she told him. 'I must spend my life making tours around the world. How could you spend your life in a stage-box admiring me?'

'You wouldn't have to make tours if we were married,' he said.

'Then what should we do?'

'We should spend our time in my house in London or at my place in the country.'

The 'place in the country' to which Paris referred, and to which he invited her to stay for three months, was Oldway House, Paignton. It had been built by his father in the early 1870s after the Franco-Prussian War dashed his hopes of retiring from New York to the French capital and made him think twice about living on the Continent. Isaac Singer died just a few weeks before the immense building was completed in August 1875. Paris, who liked to think of himself as an architect, made substantial alterations, so that the stately pile began to resemble the Palace of Versailles, not least in size, with its 115 rooms, cavernous marble entrance hall and gilded staircase. It included a theatre and hall of mirrors, as well as a ballroom with sprung floor, minstrels' gallery, Gobelin tapestry and a 30 ft long painting of Napoleon's coronation by Jacques Louis David, which was mounted on rollers and could be slid into a fireproof container. The grounds provided lawns, lakes, streams, grotto gardens and a 'riding and exercising' pavilion a little smaller than the Albert Hall for the pleasure of the Singer family and guests. Magnificent sea views had been achieved by the purchase and demolition of 20 cottages that stood in the way.

For anyone who chose to explore the world outside Oldway House, Paris offered a choice of 14 sparkling automobiles from his garage. There was also a specially built coach seating 30 people, which was pulled by eight horses. At the back of the coach was a bandstand on which the Italian Band of Torquay often played. There was no excuse for a Singer guest to be bored!

Despite her doubts about marriage, Isadora was happy to accept Paris's invitation to spend the late summer with him in Devon, discovering the joys of English country life. She was keen for other friends to join them, writing to one, 'Paris is very anxious to know if you are coming to stay with us in Panginton. . . . Do come. We will have a glorious time.'

But, as she recounts in her memoirs, the 'glorious time' did not materialize.

'I had not reckoned on the rain. In an English summer it rains all day long. The English people do not seem to mind it at all. They rise and have an early breakfast of

31

eggs and bacon, and ham and kidneys and porridge. Then they don mackintoshes and go forth into the humid country until lunch, when they eat many courses, ending with Devonshire cream. From lunch to five o'clock they are supposed to be busy with their correspondence, though I believe they really go to sleep. At five they descend to their tea, consisting of many kinds of cakes and bread and butter and tea and jam. After that they make a pretence of playing bridge, until it is time to proceed to the really important business of the day — dressing for dinner, at which they appear in full evening dress, the ladies very décolleté and the gentlemen in starched shirts, to demolish a 20 course dinner. When this is over they engage in some light political conversation, or touch upon philosophy until the time comes to retire. You can imagine whether this life pleased me or not. In the course of a couple of weeks I was positively desperate.'

Worse still, Paris had just suffered a stroke in London and was attended at Paignton by a doctor and nurse. Isadora was given a room at the opposite end of the house, being told by the doctor that on no account was she to disturb her host, who spent most of the time in his room on a diet of rice, macaroni and water. He was regularly put in a sort of cage which had been specially imported from France, in which he sat while thousands of volts of electricity were turned on him. He would sit in it patiently, looking extremely pathetic and saying: 'I hope this will do me good.' All in all, the late summer interlude was not turning out to be what Isadora had expected, and her isolation from her lover, combined with the atrocious British weather, may perhaps explain what followed.

Bored and restless, she decided to put her time to better use by practising her dancing. She telegraphed to Paris, the city in which she was currently living and performing, and asked the conductor Gabriel Pierné to arrange for somebody to come over and accompany her at the piano. The man who duly stepped down from the train at Queen's Park and was whisked away to the Singer mansion proved to be the conductor and composer André Caplet. This was about the last person she would have dreamt of choosing, though not on artistic grounds, since André, 31, was a very gifted musician, a past winner, like Berlioz and Bizet, of the Prix de Rome. No, Isadora had no complaints about his skills at the piano; what she objected to was, firstly, his ugliness and, secondly, that he already adored her. However, it seems that he was not actually ugly, but possessed such an unusual face that you either loved or loathed it. Isadora had met him once before, when he was scheduled to conduct her performance at the Théâtre de la Gaîté. It was there that he confessed that he was her slave. She rebuffed him most unkindly by telling him that she found him physically abhorrent. She also refused to have him conduct for her, demanding that Pierné take his place. She later described her feelings. 'He gave me a sense of absolute physical revulsion whenever I looked at him or touched his hand. I could do nothing against this feeling of repulsion and I simply could not stand him.'

Thus, when André arrived, she was stunned with disbelief.

'How is it possible that Pierné has sent you? He knows I hate and detest you!'

Poor André humbly begged her pardon and crept away to his room, trailing miserably in the butler's wake. When Paris was informed of his new guest's identity, he joked that he would not have any cause for jealousy.

Isadora lacked any desire to work with André, but the Devon weather broke her resistance. She began to practise dancing again, in the vast ballroom. Because it distracted her, the great tapestry was kept out of sight, and so was André — she placed a screen round him. Another of the guests, a countess, told her off for being so beastly to the Frenchman and suggested the three of them go for a drive

33

after lunch, to which Isadora reluctantly agreed. As usual, it was pouring with rain. Before long she found herself overcome with disgust at sitting next to him and tapped on the glass, indicating to the chauffeur that she wished to go home. While the chauffeur was reversing into a field, the car rocked in deep wagon ruts, throwing Isadora and André abruptly together.

'He closed his arms around me. I sat back and looked at him, and suddenly felt my whole being going up in flames like a pile of lighted straw. I have never felt anything so violent. And, all of a sudden, as I looked at him, I was aghast. How had I not seen it before? His face was perfectly beautiful, and in his eyes there was a smothered flame of genius. From that moment I knew that he was a great man. All the way back to the house I gazed at him in a kind of passionate trance, and as we entered the hall, he took my hand, and still keeping his eyes upon mine, drew me gently behind the screen in the ballroom. How was it possible that from such violent antipathy could be born such violent love?'

Like all new lovers, they were desperate to be alone together, and in a house with 115 rooms the opportunities for clandestine romance were numerous. On dry days, they lost themselves in the rambling grounds, oblivious to anything but each other. Meanwhile, under the gimlet eye of his nurse, Paris knuckled down to his macaroni, alleviated by bouts in the electric chair. But at length rumours, tittle-tattle and bits of ribald gossip reached his ears, and André was informed that his services were no longer required in Paignton. Not long after, Isadora returned to France. Her stay in Devon proved to her that domestic life was not for her.

She continued her relationship with Paris for another six years; it ended after he offered to buy her Madison Square Garden and she refused. In 1913 their son Patrick was drowned when the car he was in rolled backwards into the Seine; the Scottish nurse and Isadora's daughter died with him. Isadora was killed on the Côte d'Azur in 1927 at the age of 50, also in a motoring accident; her long scarf became entangled in the spokes of a wheel, and she was instantly throttled. Paris survived her by five years. André Caplet went on to become an international conductor, appearing at Covent Garden the year after his romance at Paignton, then being appointed to the Boston Opera. He was badly wounded and gassed in the First World War and died of lung disease in 1925. Isadora later wrote of him, 'I realised that I was right in feeling that this man was a genius — and genius has always had a fatal attraction for me'.

During the First World War, Paris converted Oldway House into a military hospital, equipping it at his own expense. In 1946 it was purchased by the local authority and made a civic centre with municipal offices and other facilities. Dances are held in the ballroom, where the Torbay Council meets every six weeks. Few other councils anywhere can enjoy such sumptuous surroundings. The building was used for the appropriate scenes in the 1968 movie *Isadora*, starring Vanessa Redgrave and Jason Robards.

The Dartmoor Massacre

DARTMOOR'S infamous prison at Princetown played host to a great variety of sinners in the last century, some of whom were certainly not the hardened criminals generally associated with this grim place. Among its most well-known early inmates was the Tichborne claimant, Arthur Orton, sentenced to 14 years for masquerading as the missing baronet Sir Roger Tichborne, heir to an annual £20,000. Though the son of a Wapping butcher, Orton seemed such a naturally charming gentleman that almost everyone believed him, including his chums in Dartmoor. Holding him to be an honest nobleman cheated of his rightful inheritance, they always addressed him as Sir Roger and sought his ruling on their disputes and arguments. He left prison in 1884 after substantial remission for exemplary conduct, went on the halls and died in 1898.

Another notable jail-bird was Charles Wells, 'the man that broke the bank at Monte Carlo.' One of the most inventive swindlers of all time — people generously funded his efforts to produce angora wool from cats — he absconded to Monte Carlo, where Scotland Yard caught up with him after he attracted notice through a series of staggering wins at the gaming table. The croupiers had to send out continuously for fresh funds as he broke the bank six times in a single day, picking up a cool £60,000. Wells was arrested on his yacht, brought back to England and ordered to exchange his 'independent air' for the chiller

36

winds of Dartmoor. He, too, proved a model prisoner, serving much less than his eight allotted years. Governor Thomson called him 'the pleasantest and the most unselfish of all the rascals that passed through my hands.'

The prison was actually erected to accommodate French sailors and soldiers captured during the Napoleonic Wars. Construction of its five basic buildings was begun in 1806 and completed three years later at a cost of £130,000. The vast blocks, each designed to take 1,500 men, were positioned radiating outwards like the spokes of a wheel, surrounded by two walls, the outer 16 ft high and a mile long. At 1,400 ft above sea level, the prison was sited in the bleakest part of Dartmoor. 'It's a real Siberia, blanketed in snow,' wrote one Frenchman. 'When the snow at last goes, the mist comes. What despotism that perfidious Albion should consign human beings to such a place!'

Why was the prison situated in 'such a place', at Princetown? The answer is that it suited the ambitions of Thomas Tyrwhitt, MP for Plymouth and Lord Warden of the Stannaries. As owner of an estate at Tor Royal, a mile south-east of Princetown, he had been trying with limited success to develop the surrounding neighbourhood. What he principally lacked was a plentiful supply of cheap labour to quarry the local granite.

Hitherto the French captives had been quartered at Plymouth in the Old Mill Prison, the Citadel and a number of rotting decrepit ships, the 'hulks', anchored mostly in the Hamoaze, at the mouth of the Tamar. These various establishments were expensive to run, offered opportunities for escape and by 1806 were completely inadequate. Tyrwhitt saw the potential in the ever-mounting numbers of able-bodied Frenchmen. He commissioned the architect Daniel Alexander to draft plans for a prison at Princetown and vigorously canvassed support for the idea among fellow politicians and friends in high places. As a result, Parliament ratified the project, and in May 1809 2,500 Frenchmen were marched the 16 miles up from Plymouth along a cart track in driving rain and through the dreaded archway on which had been inscribed a quotation from Virgil, 'Spare the vanquished'. The vanquished, who slept in hammocks, were victualled by contractors for £3,000 a year — each man's food cost the prison about a penny a day and consisted mainly of barley, bread, potatoes, cabbage and onions. The very few decent clothes they possessed were soon appropriated by the warders, so that many men were half-naked and without rug or blanket.

The prisoners increased to 8,000 and in the spring of 1813 were joined by 500 US seamen seized in the Anglo-American War of 1812–14. With the capture of Napoleon and his removal to Elba, the French were steadily released, but American numbers multiplied rapidly, so that by the end of 1814, when a treaty was concluded between Britain and the United States, they amounted to 5,000 crammed into two buildings. A US captain, Charles Andrews, recalled in his memoirs being escorted from Plymouth at 10.30 am on 2nd April 1813 to 'the depot of living death. We arrived at Dartmoor late in the afterpart of the day, and found the ground covered with snow. The prison of Dartmoor is situated on the east side of one of the highest and most barren mountains in England and is surrounded on all sides as far as the eye can see by the gloomy features of a black moor, uncultivated and uninhabited, except by one or two miserable cottages, just discernible in an eastern view, the tenants of which live by cutting turf on the moor and selling it at the prison. The place is deprived of everything that is pleasant or agreeable and is productive of nothing but human woe and misery.'

Although peace was declared at Christmas 1814, the American prisoners, swelled by then to 6,000, were still on Dartmoor the following April because the two countries could not agree over who should ship them back to the States. Becoming restless, some of them played a practical joke by attaching a jacket and trousers to a rope and lowering them slowly down one of the outside walls. The Governor, Captain Thomas Shortland, instructed a volley to be let off at the jacket and trousers before realizing he had been fooled.

Soon afterwards, on the evening of 6th April, when a small hole was discovered in a wall, Captain Shortland lost his temper and his nerve, directed the alarm bells to be rung and called out a company of the Somerset Regiment, who were on duty at Princetown. The soldiers emerged from their barracks in battle formation, drums beating. The prisoners, believing there must be a fire, poured into the yard and rushed towards the gates, which some of them managed to force. Captain Shortland ordered a bayonet charge, then told the troops to commence shooting. American men and boys fell dead or wounded, but not content with this, Captain Shortland took the soldiers to a distant corner of the yard where a poor shaking lad lay huddled against the wall. According to Charles Andrews, the bullets from five guns terminated his suffering, after which the company was returned to barracks. Seven men had been killed, seven needed amputations to save their lives, and more than 50 were severely wounded. That the casualties were so comparatively few was because most of the Somerset infantrymen could not bring themselves to aim directly at the prisoners and shot over their heads.

A formal inquiry exonerated Captain Shortland, and he continued as Governor. Yet evidence produced by the Americans suggests he had often earlier expressed his intention of 'fixing the damned rascals' before they proved too much for him. It was also held that just prior to the massacre he had been drinking heavily in Plymouth and returned in an alcoholic fury. Despite their official support for the Governor, the British Government gave compensation and pensions to the injured and the families of the dead. Captain Shortland was later appointed Commissioner of Port Royal Dockyard in Jamaica; he died there of yellow fever in 1825.

A few weeks after the massacre the first of the American prisoners were freed. But hardly had they gone, when 4,000 more Frenchmen arrived on the heels of Napoleon's escape from Elba and defeat at Waterloo. They had been shipped over from Belgium so promptly that many were still caked with blood on reaching Princetown. Napoleon's final detention in St Helena ensured their stay on Dartmoor was not a long one.

The remaining American prisoners were mainly blacks, who had continually given up their places on ships bound for the southern states lest they be taken into slavery on arrival. The last of them went on 16th February 1816. They left behind many dead comrades, not only the seven slaughtered men, but another 211 who in the space of three years had succumbed to disease, deprivation and the cold. French losses were considerably greater — over 1,200 in seven years.

Once the prisoners had gone, the Governor, his staff and the soldiers also departed, locking the gates behind them. The vast granite buildings now stood empty. Thus they remained for 31 years, battered through the seasons by wind, rain and snow, until in 1847 the British Patent Naphtha Company took a lease on the premises, then vacated them owing to bankruptcy. Finally in 1850 the Government decided to reopen the 'Princetown Depot' as a convict prison, to relieve overcrowding elsewhere.

Astonishing works of art serve as memorials to the first years of Dartmoor Prison. In Plymouth City Museum is a fascinating collection of exquisite ship models carved from bone by French prisoners of war. So skilful and accurate is the workmanship that the makers are thought to have been Paris jewellers before being conscripted. The rigging on the ships, probably executed with the help of experienced seamen, is made of human hair meticulously reeved through minute blocks and deadeyes. The delightful figureheads are so tiny that you need a magnifying glass to appreciate their details. That such work was produced, without adequate tools or light, in the dreadfully cramped conditions in which the prisoners lived is little short of a miracle. Several of the craftsmen did not stop at the completion of their ships, but built display cases for them, sometimes with as many as three mirrors at the back to give further views — and let you check that all the hundred guns are there! Models like these are now worth many thousand of pounds and are eagerly snapped up at auction.

Every year, American tourists flock to Princetown to visit the most poignant reminder of those early days, the church of St Michael and All Angels, a quarter of a mile from the prison. This was largely constructed by American and French prisoners between 1810 and 1815, and many of their countrymen are buried there. In 1910 an American women's organization, the Daughters of 1812, presented to the church a beautiful stained glass window in memory of those 'who helped to build the church; and especially of the 218 brave men who died here on behalf of their country.' If you look carefully in the church, you will also find a tablet inscribed to Thomas Tyrwhitt, 'whose name and memory are inseparable from all great works in Dartmoor'.

A
Gentleman
of the Road

THROUGHOUT the length and breadth of the West
Country, only one highwayman's name is recalled
with affection — Devon's own Tom Faggus, a 17th century
Robin Hood-like figure whose daring exploits and
breathtaking escapes in company with his wonderful
strawberry roan horse, *Winnie*, made him the archetypal
highwayman hero.

Tom's early years were spent at North Molton, twelve
miles from Barnstaple, where he earned his living as a
blacksmith — a trade at which he excelled, for he won a
prize at a North Devon show for the best-shod horse. His
forge, standing next to the old Poltimore Arms, survived
until well into the 20th century before being demolished.
When still in his twenties, he fell foul of the powerful
Bampfylde family who lived at Court Hall. Forced into a
lawsuit, he lost his case and was ruined, losing everything
he owned. This disaster sparked off another — his
imminent marriage to Betsy Paramore was cancelled by
her father. Tom was forbidden to see his sweetheart again.

Heartbroken, and raging against cruel Fate, Faggus
turned to highway robbery, achieving instant success. His
courteous behaviour, composure, and lack of violence
immediately set him apart from the gangs of surly ruffians

who terrorized the Devonshire highways. He relieved wealthy travellers of their valuables with authority and aplomb, but allowed less affluent wayfarers to pass by unmolested. This unusual conduct made him conspicuous, and he soon needed to use all his skill and ingenuity to evade the many traps laid for him. In this, he was greatly aided by his horse, *Winnie*, a most intelligent and faithful strawberry roan mare whose fantastic speed saw off many pursuers. Together they formed a formidable partnership. Once, held at gunpoint by a suspicious rider, Tom was extricated from his difficulties when *Winnie* reared up and dashed the firearm from their opponent's hand, rendering him harmless and speechless with one blow of her hoof. Tom then brandished his own pistol and gleefully pocketed the gentleman's cash.

Another time, he was relaxing with a mug of ale in a quiet corner of the Exmoor Arms in Simonsbath, while *Winnie* enjoyed her lunch in the stable. The landlord, a paltry fellow greedy for reward, knew quite well who his guests were and sent for constables. Four of them arrived just when Tom was feeling rather sleepy, and they managed to grab hold of him before he had come to his senses. Jerked into instant preparedness by the unpleasant sensation of being pinned down, he let forth a piercing whistle. From the stable came the sounds of splintering timber as *Winnie* crashed through her door. She thundered into the inn, teeth bared and eyes rolling, so terrifying Tom's captors that they decided, to a man, to make discretion the better part of valour and scrambled for the way out, tripping over each other in their haste to avoid the mare's deadly hooves. The two companions then made a leisurely and triumphant exit from the tavern.

Not long afterwards, news reached the people of Exford that Faggus was on his way there from Simonsbath. A posse of armed volunteers was gathered hurriedly together and stationed at Exford Bridge to lie in wait for him. After a nerve-racking delay they saw, looming out of the wintry morning mist, a strawberry horse and her rider. Much as they tried to discern the stranger's features, the vigilantes could not be sure it was Faggus. He, quick-witted as ever, realized that they were a bunch of ditherers and took the initiative by demanding to know for whom they were waiting. Excitedly, they told him of the famous highwayman and their plans for his capture. Tom begged to join them and of course they readily agreed. He inspected their firearms and gravely advised them to discharge the guns and reload, since the powder was damp and useless. They followed his suggestion with alacrity, firing into the air, engulfing the bridge in clouds of smoke. As the air cleared, a steely voice rang forth, requesting money from the thunderstruck posse, who found themselves staring at two unwavering loaded pistols. Collecting their purses in his hat, Tom thanked them courteously and with a cheery 'Merry Christmas to you all!' he galloped away towards Wheddon Cross.

Faggus and *Winnie* were in a more desperate situation just across the Devon border at Porlock, when a cottage in which they had taken refuge was surrounded by local people armed with anything they could get hold of — ancient firearms, pitchforks, scythes and so on. They roared and shouted in somewhat premature elation, certain he could not elude them. When they saw his hat emerging from the chimney they all fired wildly at it, each one believing that his aim was lethal. Since the headgear promptly disappeared, a satisfied yell issued from dozens of mouths, and a concerted rush was made for the cottage entrance. Before anyone reached it, the door flew open and Tom, mounted on his trusty steed, stormed out of the house and barged through their ranks, scattering them in all directions. Within seconds, he had outdistanced his persecutors and was racing back to his own county.

One of Tom's victims, stopped on the Barnstaple road, turned out to be his enemy Sir Richard Bampfylde, the man who had ruined him and wrecked his romance. With

45

shaking hands, the fat and cowardly knight proffered his well-filled purse and his jewellery. Having carefully scrutinized these items, Tom returned them, with a most courtly bow, to their owner, remarking that it was not customary for one robber to steal from another.

The most spectacular escape made by Faggus and *Winnie* took place in Barnstaple, where the highwayman was positively identified and the authorities informed. Uneasy at the amount of unfriendly interest shown in him, he resolved to leave town right away. He was aware that he was being followed as he set off towards Sticklepath, and yet, trotting on to the 16-arched bridge over the river Taw, he must have felt relieved that open country was just ahead of him. To his alarm, at the far end of the bridge was a blockade manned by constables. He glanced over his shoulder and saw that his exit was also blocked by pursuers. Trapped at last! There was only one possible way out and without a second thought he took it — he turned *Winnie* towards the parapet, and, shouting encouragement to her, urged her over the edge. The pair sailed through the air, falling 40 ft into the river. A great fountain of spray shot upwards, soaking some of his open-mouthed adversaries. The indomitable *Winnie* struck out for the shore, and as they emerged safely from the water, Tom waved his sodden hat at the constables before cantering away.

Alas, Tom and *Winnie*'s adventures came to an end at Exbridge, three miles from Dulverton. Once again, a trap was set for him, but this one had been meticulously organized. A constable, disguised as a beggar, shuffled into the tavern where Faggus was resting. With his habitual generosity to unfortunates, Tom offered to buy the man a drink, but his kindness proved his undoing. The 'beggar', choosing the right moment for his attack, knocked him to the floor. Reinforcements were on hand to hold him fast, while his ankles were tightly bound and he was hoisted to the rafters. Hanging upside down, Tom despairingly tried to whistle for *Winnie*, but the carefully laid trap included dealing with his devoted friend, and she lay dead in her stable.

The inevitable doom awaited Tom Faggus — a rough hempen rope round his neck — abruptly terminating the career of a highwayman so remarkable that he is still fondly remembered as a kind and gentle man who gave a great deal of his booty to the sick and needy folk of North Devon.

However . . . no official record of his execution has been unearthed, which allows his many admirers, past and present, to hope that perhaps, after all, he managed a final miraculous escape, even though *Winnie* was no longer able to help him. R. D. Blackmore was one of those who could hardly bear to contemplate the miserable end of our highwayman-hero. Manipulating the historical evidence just a little, he gave him a starring role in *Lorna Doone*, married him to Jan Ridd's sister Annie, and had King James II grant him a pardon. Happy endings are the best.

The
Devil's Footprints

ACCORDING to legend, the Devil has paid Devon a number of calls over the centuries and on several occasions left her inhabitants lasting tokens of his visits. His most durable souvenirs include mighty rocks flung down in fiendish rage or a fit of the sulks, like the Devil's Boulder at Shebbear, and great holes blasted out of the ground for some fell purpose, like the Devil's Limekiln on Lundy. But the most amazing mementos of the Gruesome Grockle seem to have been the footprints he left in the snow through village after village east and west of the Exe during the night of 8th February 1855.

These phenomena came as the climax of a singularly cold winter in South Devon, when the temperature fell lower than anyone could recall, and the Exe and Teign estuaries froze so solid that people could walk safely on the ice. At Bishopsteignton a boy went across the Teign with a wheelbarrow. In Exeter some merrymakers took a stove onto the river and held an impromptu party. Then, as dawn broke on the morning of Friday 9th February, early risers in Topsham, Ebford, Exton, Woodbury, Lympstone, Exmouth, Starcross, Dawlish and Teignmouth looked out of their windows to see strange tracks in the snow. Neighbour called to neighbour, and soon hundreds of people were gazing and gossiping, wondering what creature had passed by during the night. For, in an unbroken line, the tracks went down lanes, across fields, gardens, courtyards, walls, haystacks, even over rooftops. Mile upon mile of identical prints were clearly visible on both sides of the Exe estuary in a seemingly endless trail. In Lympstone there was hardly a garden in which the creature had not left its mark. *Woolmer's Exeter and Plymouth Gazette* reported:

'Its track appears more like that of a biped than a quadruped, and the steps are generally eight inches in advance of each other, though in some cases twelve or 14, and are alternate like the steps of a man, and would be included between two parallel lines six inches apart. The impression of the foot closely resembles that of a donkey's shoe, and measures from an inch and a half to (in some cases) two inches and a half across, here and there appearing as if the foot was cleft, but in the generality of its steps the impression of the shoe was continuous and perfect; in the centre the snow remains entire, merely showing the outer crust of the foot, which, therefore, must have been convex. The creature seems to have advanced to the doors of several houses, and then to have retraced its steps, but no one is able to discern the starting or resting point of this mysterious visitor. Everyone is wondering, but no one is able to explain the mystery; the poor are full of superstition, and consider it little short of a visit from old Satan or some of his imps ... I observed the impressions of my horse's foot made on the same night, and found they measured more than six inches across, whereas the real measurement of the foot was four and a half. This, no doubt, arose from the footprint forming a nidus for the rain, which, by thawing, expanded the foot to its exaggerated size. I think it therefore difficult to arrive at the precise size of the animal's foot, which would, doubtless, be influenced by the same cause.'

In Dawlish, like Lympstone, the tracks seemed to be everywhere and were thought to resemble those of a donkey, though in some instances they appeared cloven. Many townsfolk became so agitated that a posse was raised which spent most of Friday hunting the beast with guns and bludgeons. They gathered in the churchyard of St Gregory's, then followed the footprints out to Luscombe Castle, along Dawlish Water and eventually back to Oaklands Park, but all to no avail.

Numerous people who had seen the tracks considered them to be produced by a large bird from a foreign country; others felt they could be those of a wolf or an animal that had escaped from a travelling menagerie. But there was a growing suspicion that they were the fleeting, perhaps unintentional, evidence of a nocturnal romp by the Devil himself. Certainly they tallied with traditional fancies about the size and shape of demonic feet, and they marched along as if made by something or someone walking on two legs.

The tracks were so widely feared to be the Devil's that on the following Sunday when the Rev George Musgrave of Withycombe Raleigh preached in Lympstone church, he alluded to the mysterious visitor, saying that, though Satan was continuously abroad, he was invisible and a more subtle, dangerous individual than the poor creature who had hopped through the snow. Mr Musgrave, the first scholar to render the Hebrew Psalter into English blank verse, thought the animal was probably a kangaroo.

Other suggestions as to identity included otters, rats, badgers, large birds driven ashore by the weather, and a rope trailing from a hot-air balloon.

During the next few weeks discussions and arguments raged not only in Devon, but throughout the national press. Both *The Times* and *The News of the World* devoted lengthy articles to the subject, while the *Illustrated London News* featured it in four successive issues, from 24th February to 17th March.

Correspondents presented various theories. The most balanced opinion came from a man who had spent a long winter in the backwoods of Canada and so was familiar with every type of bird and animal track. He concluded that no proper explanation had been offered, nor was it ever likely to be; nothing in his experience could produce such a print in a straight line. He admitted that he was completely baffled by the way in which the prints removed the snow underneath as cleanly as a branding iron. The possibility that the creature therefore must have had red-hot feet did nothing to reassure those already half-convinced of a devilish manifestation.

Day by day, the weather grew warmer and a steady thaw set in. The footmarks, greatly disturbed by the large numbers of sightseers, disappeared quite rapidly, and no new ones were spotted. Gradually the hubbub died down, the newsmen lost interest, and life returned to normal in South Devon. On 6th March *The Times* decided 'the matter at present is as much involved in mystery as ever it was.' To this day, no satisfactory explanation of the riddle has been put forth. Only those who believed that it really was Old Nick himself were content, and no-one has been able to prove them wrong.

They know that he prances around the county quite undetected most of the time, although he makes his presence felt on 20th September every year. This is the day when he spits on the blackberries, making them inedible. After that, only maggots enjoy eating them.

51

The King of the Beggars

BAMPFYLDE Moore Carew, born at Bickleigh, near Tiverton, in July 1690, came from one of the West Country's premier families, many of whom had been knighted for services to the State. His father, the rector of Bickleigh, sent him to Blundell's School, Tiverton, from which scholars traditionally progressed to Exeter College, Oxford. Young Carew decided otherwise. Though good at Greek and Latin, he ran away from school in his fifth year and was not seen again for 18 months, when he turned up on his parents' doorstep. He had spent the time with gipsies, living by his wits and learning the craft of begging.

He stayed at home for a while, then disappeared again, returning to the gipsies. Soon he was skilled enough in begging and confidence tricks to venture into the world alone as a fully fledged vagabond. A master of disguise, he made a profitable tour of South Devon posing as a pathetic shipwrecked mariner. Finishing at Totnes, he journeyed to Exeter and, wearing only a blanket, became an equally successful madman. He thereafter appeared variously as a miller whose mill had been destroyed by fire; a farmer whose cattle had been drowned in the floods; a clergyman who resigned his living as a matter of conscience over swearing allegiance to the government; a peg-legged tinner disabled in the mines, with wife, seven children and 'pity-moving beard'; and a widow whose family were burned to death at Crediton. He once presented himself to some friends three times in a row in three different disguises, obtaining money on each occasion without exciting the slightest suspicion. Pretending to be an authority on buried treasure, he charged a woman 20 guineas for telling her that a fortune lay beneath the roots of a laurel tree in her garden.

He was a terrific opportunist. When the loss of a vessel was reported in a neighbourhood, he would arrive there as the only survivor. At Stoke Gabriel, near Dartmouth, the vicar sat him in the front pew of St Gabriel's and made the congregation donate a generous collection as recompense for his tribulations. Once while passing through a seaside town, he heard of a ship being driven on the rocks. He ran down the beach, stripped off his clothes and swam out to the vessel, which by then had foundered. After learning from a dying sailor details of the voyage and the captain's name, he swam back to shore, where he was comforted by sympathetic villagers. Welcomed into one of their homes, he convalesced for several days before departing with a substantial bounty contributed by the community. Similarly, when he heard about a fire and could reach it in time, he would discover information and names of some of the casualties, one of whom he would impersonate with blackened face and singed clothes.

He liked to play the role of religious madman — Quaker, Wesleyan, Nonconformist, Roman Catholic — shouting, raving, chanting in Greek and Latin with such fervour that even the Bishop of Bath and Wells, Dr John Wynne, felt compelled to offer him half-a-crown. He would also visit churchyards, look for a recent tombstone, study its inscription, then, dressed as a clergyman, call on the deceased's family and improvise an emotive means to relieve them of some of their inheritance.

He occasionally travelled outside the West Country and

in Newcastle met Mary Gray, daughter of a surgeon. She went back to Devon with him; they were married at Stoke Damerel, Plymouth, in December 1733.

With a wife and a little girl to support, he was forced often to be away from them, earning his living. He began to take more risks and in February 1739 was arrested for the first time. Eagle-eyed Justice Lethbridge apprehended him in Barnstaple a few days after an encounter on Pilton Bridge when Carew, disguised as a cripple, had evaded capture by inciting the Justice's horse to bolt. He was taken to Exeter and held until the Quarter Sessions in the Castle on 1st May. No detailed charge was preferred, but, quoting a 1714 statute in respect to vagabondage, Judge Richard Beavis pronounced him a dangerous and incorrigible rogue. After a further six months in prison, he was handed over to an Exeter merchant, Ethelred Davy, who shipped him from Falmouth to Talbot County, Maryland — even though no transportation order had been issued. Negotiations for his sale as a slave were underway when he escaped, but he was quickly recaptured and had a heavy iron collar riveted round his neck. He managed to get away again, finding unexpected sanctuary among a tribe of Red Indians who looked after him and sawed off the collar.

Before long, he set off north to New Castle, Pennsylvania, then to New London, Connecticut, portraying himself as a victimized Quaker, thereby raising the money for a passage home. When his ship docked at Bristol, he avoided the unwelcome attentions of the press-gang by feigning smallpox, pricking his arms and chest and rubbing in salt and gunpowder.

His return journey through Somerset and Devon was like a royal progress: squires, parsons, doctors and farmers showered him with hospitality, so great was his fame. The aristocracy also admired Carew, seeing him as a man of breeding who possessed the courage and imagination to seek a life of adventure, heedless of its perils. He counted among his friends the Earl of Anglesey, Lord Weymouth,

Sir William Wyndham, Sir William Courtenay of Powderham Castle and his close relations Lord Clifford of Chudleigh, Sir Henry Carew and Sir Coventry Carew. He was aware of his status. Begging once outside a doctor's house with a like-minded companion, he contemptuously refused the halfpenny proffered by a maidservant. Passing it to his colleague, he remarked to the girl, 'Tell your master I am not a halfpenny man, but Bampfylde Moore Carew, the King of the Beggars.' The doctor shortly came to the door with his daughter and gave him sixpence and a mug of drink. Carew thanked him, chatted equably for a while, then took his leave.

Soon after his return to Devon, he was strolling with his wife along the quay in Exeter when he was spotted by the merchant, Ethelred Davy, who had illegally transported him to America. Some of Davy's men grabbed him, bundled him onto a ship and chained him in the hold, threatening Mary Carew with dire consequences if she dared go to the authorities. Carew had reappeared in England so quickly that Davy first thought the vessel on which he dispatched him had not completed its voyage. Though pleased to find it had reached its destination, he safeguarded future business transactions with the County Court by sending Carew back to the colonies posthaste on his next ship to cross the Atlantic. However, Carew responded to this second transportation as he had done to the first, and within a few months he was in Boston, acquiring the necessary funds for a return passage.

In 1747 he was arrested again, committed to Southgate in Exeter for six months and whipped four times round Castle Green. Two years later he collaborated with Robert Goadby, proprietor of the *Sherborne Mercury*, to produce *The Life and Adventures of Bampfylde Moore Carew, the King of the Beggars*. This book proved so successful that it was reprinted several times, establishing Carew, to this day, as the most famous of all English beggars. Robert Goadby's wife, Rachel, is thought to have done the actual writing, describing her subject as 'tall and majestic, his limbs strong and well proportioned, his features regular, his countenance open and ingenuous.'

A little later, he abandoned the career which he had graced with such talent and originality. One source suggests that, consumed by remorse over wicked deeds, he suffered severe illness, precipitating retirement financed by his relative Sir Thomas Carew of Haccombe, near Newton Abbot, who was MP for Minehead. Another source maintains that, having pretended so often to be a clergyman, he began to think like one. Meditating once on St Luke 12:48, 'For unto whomsoever much is given, of him shall be much required', he experienced such pangs of guilt that he forthwith called it a day. He is also said to have won £9,000 in a lottery and lived out his remaining years at Bickleigh in great comfort. He died in June 1758 and was buried at the south-east end of his father's church, St Mary's, where he had been christened 68 years earlier.

> 'King Carew's race at length is run,
>   His wanderings are all o'er;
> No more his tricks, nor wit, nor fun,
>   Will make the table roar.'

The
Curse
of Coppinger

As the full fury of the storm hit the rocky north-western tip of Devon at Hartland Point, huge Atlantic breakers crashed onto the treacherous razor-sharp reef which formed its shore. In the midst of this hellish turmoil, an ill-fated ship, blown off course, was being torn inexorably to pieces. The cracking of her timbers and the terrified screams of her doomed crew were just faintly heard above the din by the watchers gathering near the shore. Surely it was impossible for anybody to survive! And yet, looming out of the boiling surf, a massive figure could be seen struggling inch by inch to safety. The watchers gazed in wonder as he staggered up the beach. Cruel Coppinger had come ashore.

'Will you hear of the Cruel Coppinger?
He came from a foreign kind:
He was brought to us by the salt water,
He was carried away by the wind.'

The high drama of Coppinger's arrival in Devon 'by the salt water' did not end when he stood naked and dripping on the land. Without a word, he snatched a thick red cloak from the shoulders of an old woman and wrapped himself in it. Majestically, he marched across the pebbles to a girl mounted on a fine horse, leapt up behind her, grabbed the reins and urged the surprised beast into a gallop. In a few moments they were lost to view. An excited babble broke out among the watchers, who had stood mesmerized while Coppinger helped himself to clothing, transport, and a woman.

They thought he was a hero. He became a curse — a figure of legend, steeped in savagery, glorying in his nickname 'Cruel Coppinger'.

He battened on the parents of the girl on the horse, using a generous offer of hospitality in their home at Galsham to win the affections of the girl, Dinah Hamlyn. She had never known anyone like him in her life and was very soon in his power, believing herself deeply in love. The natural anxieties of her parents were soothed by his tale of being from a wealthy Danish family. He said he had left his homeland to avoid an arranged marriage with a titled lady whom he could not love. Dinah's parents swallowed his story and professed themselves delighted to accept him as a prospective son-in-law.

Before long, Mr Hamlyn was stricken with a mysterious illness from which he speedily, perhaps conveniently, died. Coppinger assumed the mantle of head of the household with little fuss, marrying Dinah shortly after her father's funeral. Now, firmly in control of the property, his true nature, so long held in check, began to reveal itself. The house became the meeting-place for all the rogues in the area, and many nights were spent in wild drinking and roistering while his wife and mother-in-law cowered in their bedrooms. He organized a gang of wreckers and smugglers whose lawlessness and violence terrorized the neighbourhood. In those days, near the end of the 18th century, the parish of Hartland — all 17,000 acres of it — was isolated and remote, so that for a man of Coppinger's brilliant organizational skills it was an extremely simple matter to use his bully boys to cow the peaceable

59

inhabitants into submission and control the area as he desired.

He established regular smuggling runs to and from France and the Channel Islands, frequently leading the expedition in his own new schooner, *Black Prince*. He took the lion's share of the profits and used them to buy large tracts of land edging the sea. On one occasion the purchase of a piece of land was effected in a very unconventional way — Coppinger pouring out on the solicitor's desk a stream of foreign currency and leaving him to evaluate its worth. His shrewd acquisitions gave him exclusive use of many of the coastal pathways, which were known as 'Coppinger's Tracks'. Along these tracks came men laden with contraband, careless of the law. Just one voice was raised timidly in protest — a local parson whose unwise outburst was stifled by a severe beating from Coppinger's double-thonged whip.

Coppinger enjoyed using his whip, especially on his wife, who was regularly bound to their bedpost and lashed when her sadistic husband wanted money from his mother-in-law. He threatened to flay Dinah alive when Mrs Hamlyn objected to handing over her savings. Under these terrible conditions the two women existed from day to day. Dinah's only consolation was her baby son, a fine healthy boy on whom she lavished all her affection. But soon, she discovered he was deaf and dumb. It also began to dawn on her that from his father he had inherited the vicious nature and ungovernable temper that led the boy, when six, to push a playmate to his death over the clifftop. The knowledge that she had given birth to such a child completely shattered her. Her love for Coppinger and his brat was finally extinguished.

Coppinger, meanwhile, had tired not only of his wife and son, but of the West Country as well. His decision to seek a new base for his operations was hastened by the fact that at last the forces of law and order were beginning to mass against him. His departure from Hartland was as

THE CURSE OF COPPINGER

dramatic as his arrival. Once again, a violent thunderstorm was raging as a brig stood in as close as she dared to the shore to pick him up. She sent in a rowing boat on a perilous journey to the rocks on which he stood waiting. He leapt in and urged the rowers back through the waves towards his ship. A watcher on the cliffs, 350 ft above, saw Coppinger's last act of cruelty as he slashed with his cutlass at a sailor drooping from exhaustion. Within minutes they had boarded the ship and she dropped out of sight like a ghost. At the moment of his departure a fireball smashed through the roof of his house and landed at the foot of his chair.

'Will you hear of the Cruel Coppinger?
He came from a foreign kind:
He was brought to us by the salt water,
He was carried away by the wind.'

The stories about Coppinger and his life of crime in the West Country were gathered together by the eccentric Plymouth-born vicar of Morwenstow and Welcombe, Robert Stephen Hawker. He was a man of endless creativity who adored playing practical jokes, and it has been suggested that the 'Cruel Coppinger' legend sprang entirely from his fertile imagination. However, if this was so, he would hardly have bothered to write to his brother-in-law John Somers James in 1866, 'Do you remember Bold Coppinger the Marsland Pirate? . . . I am collecting materials for his life for *All the Year Round*. If you know any anecdotes of him or Dinah his wife, will you let me know.'

After Hawker's death in 1875, some other facts about Coppinger emerged. It was discovered that a survivor of a wreck at Welcombe Mouth had been called Daniel Herbert Coppinger and that he had been offered shelter by a nearby farmer. A few months later, he married a Miss Hamlyn in Hartland parish church. At Galsham Farm, a

61

windowpane with Coppinger's signature clearly scratched on it remained intact until 1916.

So, Coppinger *did* exist, and this undesirable temporary West Country resident inspired another extraordinary Devon clergyman, Sabine Baring-Gould (who wrote *Onward, Christian Soldiers*), to cast him as the romantic anti-hero of his novel *In the Roar of the Sea*, published in 1892 and still popular a century later.

The
Exeter
Theatre Disaster

THE introduction of gas lighting, with its warm glow, its power to create shimmering magical scenes, contributed vitally to the theatre's increased popularity during the 19th century. A marked expansion in the size of auditoriums, providing cheaper seats, also led to larger audiences. Yet, with these advances came a heavy death toll from fire. Often, by good fortune, theatres such as London's *Alhambra*, in 1882, were gutted after the evening's show had finished, and no lives were lost. In Exeter on 5th September 1887, though, it was a different story: 186 died in a disaster unparalleled in the history of the English stage.

Exeter's *New Theatre Royal*, at the junction of Longbrook Street and the New North Road (behind Debenhams) first opened its doors in October 1886, replacing the *Theatre Royal* at Bedford Circus, destroyed by fire in 1885. For eleven months, the theatre prospered. On the evening of Monday 5th September a romantic drama by George Sims, *Romany Rye*, was introduced to a packed house. There were some 600 theatregoers in the pit, 300 in the gallery, and about a hundred more in the circle and stalls. The first three acts ran very successfully for the theatre company, the stagehands coping admirably with much complicated

scene-changing, and the audience was obviously enjoying the show. Just after ten o'clock, the fourth act was well under way, and the second scene, taking place on board ship, passed smoothly. The third scene began with the leading actor, Frederick Mouillet, front-stage. In the middle of his speech, the act-drop suddenly unrolled with a bang behind him. After a startled pause, the merry theatregoers burst into laughter at the mishap. Mouillet blithely resumed, neither he nor they realizing that the evening's entertainment was about to come to an abrupt and terrible end. For at the next moment the act-drop started to bulge forward, as tongues of flame and clouds of smoke escaped from behind it. Shouts of 'Fire!' were heard on all sides, and a headlong rush for the exits began. In an incredibly short time the whole theatre — stage, boxes, galleries — was a mass of flames and suffocating smoke. To make matters worse, the gas-jets went out, throwing the auditorium into complete darkness.

Those fortunates seated in the boxes, stalls and upper circle escaped fairly easily. But in the most crowded part of the theatre — the gallery — frightful panic broke out. There was just one way out of here, via a corridor and stairs leading to the street, but the exit was soon blocked by dozens of terrified men, women and children all struggling to negotiate a narrow corridor with two sharp turns in it. Worse still, the corridor was partially barred by a ticket booth overturned in the stampede. Soon, the first fatalities, crushed and trampled to death, provided an even more effective barrier. Blazing timbers fell on the dead and dying, adding to the carnage.

In another part of the theatre the stage manager, Mr Graham, was doing his best to shepherd people to safety. He found a little girl huddled on the stairs in a smoke-filled passage. He caught hold of her and carried her downstairs. They had almost reached the bottom when a great burst of flame blew them both right into the street. He suffered severe burns to his face and hands but managed to protect the child, who was quite unharmed. Graham had been in the wings as the fire started way up above him, the naked fishtail gaslights igniting the densely-packed canvas scenery suspended over the stage. The two men working in the flies died very quickly.

Outside the theatre, a gathering crowd watched in horror as screaming women, some clutching children, streamed onto the balcony over the front entrance. Although ladders were soon in place against the walls, some could not wait and hurled themselves over the balcony onto the road to escape the scorching heat. Dreadful injuries resulted from these falls. Meanwhile, fire engines began to arrive from all over Exeter. The blaze could be seen as far away as Topsham, where the local brigade set out for the city, pulling the engine by hand in the absence of their horse. As the various fire engines approached the fire, they had to contend with four dozen of Thomas Pickford's panic-stricken horses which were kept next to the theatre and were released in case the fire spread to their stables.

An eye-witness watching the arrival of the firefighters described a scene in which 'the utmost confusion reigned supreme. The venerable turncocks were not long in coming, it is true; but the firemen seemed unable to decide which fire-plug to use. The brigade from the Higher Barracks seemed to be puzzled as to where or how to begin. . . . I give the policemen who manned the escape credit for their activity when at last the machine was brought to the point where it was most needed, but it arrived too late to be of much service in rescuing the people confined in the gallery, who had already been suffocated or burnt to death. . . . But one thing of all others that struck me was the utter incapacity of the extinguishing appliances, even to check the fire at any part of the building. The jets of water rarely reached the top of the building, the water in many cases being thrown against the outside wall of the building, and consequently failing in its effect.'

Captain Showers, the Chief Constable, was on the scene by 10.30 pm, directing the rescue operation. At around one o'clock in the morning the firemen had at last pumped enough water into the building to work their way inside. The injured, carried out on stretchers, were taken immediately to the hospital in Magdalen Street (now the West of England Eye Infirmary). Numerous people were found asphyxiated by the theatre's fire-extinguishers, which exploded with the heat and proved fatally toxic. Rescuers soon came across the pitiful heap of charred corpses of those trying to escape from the gallery. In another corridor safety could have been reached by way of a half right turn. Death came to many who, seeing no indication whatsoever, ran straight on into the restaurant, from which there was no escape. The dead were removed to the London Hotel yard opposite the theatre. Over 100 bodies were brought out, but also some ghastly remains — skulls, trunks and limbs utterly unrecognizable and impossible to identify. The death toll eventually reached 186.

Miraculously, the whole theatre company survived the blaze; their manager, Mr Russell Rosse, attributed their good fortune at least in part to lack of panic, allowing all to escape safely. The last member of the company to leave was Mr Herberte, and as he was being helped down the ladder by policemen there was a violent explosion just above him followed by a shower of burning debris.

There were two heroes of the catastrophe, both military men. Able Seaman William Hunt went back and forth into the inferno and made more than a score of daring rescues. Bombardier Scattergood of the Royal Artillery also made repeated forays into the doomed theatre to save the lives of others, regardless of his own safety. He was eventually overcome by the flames and perished. His fearfully blackened remains were found on the stairs which had been a deathtrap for so many.

As the night wore on, the streets outside the gutted

theatre were thronged with frantic people searching for relatives and friends missing in the blaze. Those who could summon up enough courage went to look for them among the rows of corpses in the London Hotel yard. The sight was ghastly. Many of the dead had faces terribly convulsed or were quite beyond recognition. Sixty bodies lay all next day awaiting identification. Worse still was the pile of bones and cinders said to represent about 30 more victims.

At nine o'clock on Tuesday morning the Town Council gathered. Shocked and stricken by the night's events, they spent a little while expressing their feelings of horror and sadness before settling down to decide on the practical help needed for the victims' relatives. A public subscription list was opened to which £400 was immediately contributed. The fund finally reached just over £20,000, which included £100 from Henry Irving and a similar amount from the Queen. Most of the money helped to support the 98 children orphaned by the disaster, like the six surviving Benellick children from Coombe Street, who lost not only father and mother, but eldest brother and sister as well.

Two days later, the sombre business of interment began. The victims were buried at the Polsloe Park cemetery on Thursday 8th September. The 68 who were identifiable had separate coffins, the remains of the other 118 being placed in 15 communal coffins. The ceremonies were attended by 10,000 people, the largest proportion of whom followed the cortège of Bombardier Scattergood.

Funeral rites were simultaneously carried out all over the cemetery that afternoon, the air reverberating with 'Man that is born of a woman hath but a short time to live and is full of misery' and the particularly pathetic 'Earth to earth, ashes to ashes, dust to dust.' But one service took an entirely unexpected turn when the mourners set upon Rev John Ingle, rector of St Olave's, Fore Street, who gave every impression of being drunk. Leading his procession to the graveside, he lurched along a zig-zag course that was remarked by many whom they passed. Beside the grave, he swayed about all over the place, made three attempts to read from his Prayer Book, but could produce only a strange sort of low mumbling. After lapsing into silence, he staggered off in the direction from which they had arrived. Several mourners shouted, 'Come back! You haven't finished the service!' He stopped, gabbled something incoherent, then pursued his wobbly path. The mourners followed, yelling and hissing, closed round him brandishing sticks and umbrellas, and the next moment he was on the ground.

At this point Sergeant-Major Whiteway of the Devonshire Regiment, who had been observing the strange sequence of events, stepped in, gathered up the rector and took him into the nearby chapel. They were joined by Rev W. G. Mallet of St Mary Major (now demolished), Cathedral Yard. After half an hour Rev Mallet and Sergeant-Major Whiteway marched Rev Ingle out of the chapel in tight formation, enduring abuse and jeers before putting him safely into a cab.

Five days later, the rector appeared before magistrates at Exeter Castle, charged with being drunk while conducting a burial service. He explained that his odd way of walking was due to sudden sharp twinges of gout in his ankles. He said he did complete the service, for he started reading it on the way to the grave. His behaviour at the cemetery was the result of recent severe illness, followed by going to see the bodies laid out in the yard of the London Hotel, which so shocked him that he could not sleep for the next two nights. The scene at the cemetery proved equally harrowing, with row upon row of open graves. Against this defence were set the opinions of Rev Mallet and Sergeant-Major Whiteway that he was indeed drunk. The Bench, feeling there was sufficient doubt, dismissed the case.

There is no point in speculating whether Rev Ingle was drunk or not. What seems beyond doubt is that the disaster affected him as dreadfully as it must have done thousands of other Exonians.

Bishop Phillpotts
and the
Sporting Parsons

Henry Phillpotts, born in Bridgwater in 1778, was Bishop of Exeter from 1831 until his death in Torquay in 1869 at the age of 91. A man of great mental powers and force of will, he was a belligerent controversialist and stern disciplinarian. He needed to be, for his clergy were among the most wayward and difficult in the country.

His great intellect was more than a match for his clergy in matters of dogma, but against a certain breed of parsons, whom he seems never before to have encountered, he proved surprisingly ineffectual. These were the sporting parsons, whose ideas of good clerical behaviour were so far removed from his own as to be incomprehensible to him. Shortly after his arrival in Devon he was driving with his chaplain to a confirmation when a fox hunt thundered past. 'Dear me!' he remarked. 'What a number of black coats among the hunters. Has there been some great bereavement in the neighbourhood?' The chaplain diffidently explained that the black-coated gentlemen were clergy. 'Their only bereavement is not being able to appear in pink.'

At that time a hundred Devon parsons hunted three days a week; some hunted six days. Twenty kept their own packs of hounds. Hunt meetings and news were announced from the pulpit. Sunday service would be cancelled if a parson wanted to ride to hounds that day. One parson, who also shot, closed his church for three months during the shooting season.

Hunting was practised with fanatical intensity. Sometimes a stag would be chased for hours before being torn apart by the hounds. One such animal covered 26 miles between discovery in Bratton Fleming, pursuit across Exmoor and death in the rectory grounds at Luccombe. Sometimes they were killed jumping from the cliffs on Devon's north coast in a desperate attempt to evade the relentless pursuers, both canine and human, baying for blood.

Exmoor, of course, was a popular hunting area, and foremost among its huntsmen at the time of Bishop Phillpotts' installation was Rev John Froude of Knowstone, who was born there in 1777 and succeeded his father as vicar in 1804, serving for 49 years. He owned a large amount of land around Knowstone and had a healthy income. Although educated at Blundell's and Oxford, he was no gentleman. By reason of his wealth and position, he developed into a sort of Mafia boss employing henchmen to harass his neighbours. According to a colleague, Rev W. H. Thornton, these ruffians 'beat the covers when he shot, they found hares for his hounds to hunt, they ran on his errands, they were the terror of the countryside. He never paid them anything, or spared or sheltered them from punishment. Sometimes they were in gaol and sometimes out. They could always have as much bacon, potatoes, bread and cheese and cider at his house as they pleased, as well as a fire to sit by or a rough bed to lie down upon. Plantations were burned, horses mutilated, chimneys choked. . . .'

Trewman's Exeter Flying-Post was constantly reporting crimes in the Knowstone area. In 1829, fields of wheat and barley were destroyed. Soon afterwards 'the property of

71

Sir C. Throgmorton was discovered to be on fire, which raged with uncontrollable fury till five acres were consumed.' Then sheep were slaughtered, ricks reduced to ashes, pet dogs dismembered. In January 1834, in an act of defiant retribution by long-suffering parishioners, the vicarage was set on fire, but the flames were extinguished before much damage had been done. Knowstone, said the *Flying-Post*, 'has for some time been the scene of almost innumerable depredations.' At the end of that year an attempt was made to murder Froude. An unknown assailant fired a gun into his bedroom but unfortunately missed him, strafing a bedpost and demolishing a mirror instead.

Froude hunted three days a week, shot on three and took Sunday services when he felt like it, often preaching to empty pews. His pack of hounds was among the finest in the West Country. It is hardly surprising he was one of the earliest whom Bishop Phillpotts arranged to visit. Communication by letter had proved very disappointing for the poor bishop. After he had enquired of Froude how many candidates were being prepared for confirmation, the reply from Knowstone arrived on the back of a list of dogs ill with distemper, stating that there were none: nobody had passed the preliminary test of reciting the Lord's Prayer backwards! When Phillpotts first tried to call on Froude, his carriage sank in a specially dug hole in a stream that crossed the road approaching the vicarage. At the next attempt he got through, but was told the 'passon' was upstairs in bed, very poorly. The bishop was frankly sceptical of this information and fired questions at Froude's housekeeper who eventually blurted out that the master had typhus. Phillpotts offered his commiserations and speedily departed, never to return. Froude died at the ripe age of 75.

Froude's nephew, Rev John Radford of Lapford, near Chawleigh, was a sporting cleric who caused Bishop Phillpotts even more bother. He had no need of henchmen

— he let his own granite fists do the talking, leaving those who had the cheek to cross him sprawling on the ground. But such triumphs were not enough; he suffered from pugilomania and needed almost daily combat. He was a huge man with a chest of 54 inches and arms like tree trunks. On Saturday evenings he would dress in bottle-green jacket, red waistcoat, corduroy breeches, worsted socks and stout boots and go into Exeter looking for fights. He knocked all his opponents senseless, usually ending the night stupefied with drink and loaded onto a cart heading for Lapford. When the railway was being extended from Crediton to Barnstaple he would appear among the navvies at work between Lapford Cross and Nymet Bridge and offer money to anyone who could beat him. Those who took up the challenge were usually laid flat as the railway track.

After the Barnstaple line started operating, he would board the market trains and pick fights with farmers, many of whom decided to return to horse and cart. He also invaded gipsy encampments holding up a sovereign as wager for the man who could defeat him. Sometimes a dozen challengers were spreadeagled before his needs were satisfied. When fairs arrived in local towns such as South Molton, he would make for the boxing booths and thrash the travelling prize-fighters. At a fair in Taunton he took the place of the beaten champ, pulverizing all comers.

Rev Radford had scant interest in his church or that at Nymet Rowland, where he also held office. During Sunday morning service his horse would be stalled in the vestry, while his hounds waited in the churchyard. His parishioners asked Bishop Phillpotts to remove him, but Radford had inherited the advowson, and little could be done. After knocking out a constable who tried serving a writ for debt on him, he was sent to prison for a month, which enabled Phillpotts to suspend him and put his curate in his place. Not long after Radford's release, the curate was found dead in bed with his throat cut. Radford was taken to Exeter and minutely questioned, but nothing could be proved against him. When he returned to Lapford, his congregation deserted him, and he took services, often ceaselessly weeping, with only his sexton in attendance. He died soon afterwards in 1861 aged 62. Like his uncle, he was used as a character in R. D. Blackmore's *The Maid of Sker*.

The most famous of Bishop Phillpotts' sporting parsons was Rev Jack Russell, born at Dartmouth in 1795. Like Froude and Radford, he went to Blundell's and Oxford, and like them, too, he was the son of a parson. Indeed, it was his father who first fell foul of Phillpotts when he infringed the 72nd canon by trying to cast out devils. One of his parishioners in Crediton believed himself to be a cider press — hardly an unworthy aspiration — and took to spinning round emitting squeaks. Russell senior's mistake was to attempt to exorcise him without consulting his bishop.

Jack Russell was so keen on hunting that he kept hounds even when a schoolboy at Blundell's, kennelling them with a local blacksmith in Tiverton. He bought his first terrier, Trump, from a milkman in Oxford; she was the ancestor of all those dogs which he bred so distinctively over the next 60 years. As a matter of interest, she and her immediate descendants had much longer legs than today's Jack Russells, whose shortness and limited speed might not have satisfied Russell's demands during a strenuous day's hunting on Exmoor.

Parson Jack became vicar of Swimbridge, five miles from Barnstaple, in 1833 and remained there 46 years, moving to Black Torrington two years before he died. He was a far finer minister than his colleague Froude, whose hunting skills he admired, though not the man. He once rebuked Froude at length in front of several other huntsmen for his foul language. Later that day Froude, bent on revenge, waylaid him in a narrow lane between high hedges. 'Who hath made thee into a lecturing bishop like melord

74

Veel-the-pot?' he cried, lashing a heavy hunting crop across his opponent's head and back, immediately drawing blood. Russell leapt from his horse, seized Froude and pulled him down into the mud where they wrestled until Russell sat astride him, pinning his shoulders and demanding an apology. It was in that position that another homegoing huntsman came across them, so they silently remounted and went their separate ways.

Bishop Phillpotts was not long in visiting Russell, slipping into one of his Sunday morning services and being surprised at the high quality of the sermon. He remarked on it afterwards to a lady worshipper. 'Yes, Mr Russell is very good in the pulpit', she agreed, 'but you should see him in the saddle!' Phillpotts requested Russell to give up his pack of hounds.

'Do you ask it as a personal favour?'

'Yes, Mr Russell, as a personal favour.'

'Very well, my lord, I will.'

'Thank you,' said the bishop.

'But I won't deceive you,' Russell added. 'Mrs Russell will keep the pack instead of me.'

His feats in the saddle became legendary. At 79 he hunted all one week around Ivybridge, then at two o'clock on the Saturday afternoon set out home across Dartmoor. Having covered the 60 miles in nine hours, he ate a hearty supper and retired to bed. Next day he took three services in his parish.

Late in life he came to the attention of the Prince of Wales, with whom he stayed at Sandringham over Christmas in 1873, going again in 1876. In 1879 the Prince hunted on Exmoor, when a stag was killed in the Doone Valley. Russell travelled up Porlock Hill with Edward in the royal carriage. He died four years later at the age of 87. The crowd at his funeral was so vast that a thousand people stood outside in the churchyard. One of the mourners remarked, 'He wasn't much of a parson, you know, in the way of visiting and suchlike. But he was such a man to make peace in a parish.'

Boney
Bows Out

O N 15th July 1815, a month after his defeat at
Waterloo, Napoleon Bonaparte went on board the
English frigate *Bellerophon*, which lay in the harbour at
Rochefort, south-west France, and surrendered to Captain
Frederick Maitland. He imagined he might be permitted to
go to America or even be granted sanctuary in England.
When HMS *Bellerophon* dropped anchor in Tor Bay on
24th July to await instructions, his hopes began to fade as
he heard for the first time that his final destination could be
the remote island of Saint Helena in the South Atlantic.

He nevertheless retained his composure and charm,
remarking to Captain Maitland while gazing towards
Torquay and Paignton, 'What a beautiful country! It very
much resembles the Bay of Portoferraio in Elba.' Word soon
spread along the coast that the fabled ex-Emperor was in Tor
Bay, and innumerable boats brought people to glimpse a man
so steeped in mystery and legend that few folk ever dreamt
they would actually set eyes on him. Of course, most children
hoped they certainly would not. 'Eat up your greens, or
Boney will get you!' and similar threats, had already struck
terror into the hearts of thousands of English tots.

During the afternoon of 25th July, as Captain Maitland
later wrote, Napoleon 'walked above an hour on deck,
frequently stood at the gangway, or opposite to the
quarter-deck ports, for the purpose of giving the people an
opportunity of seeing him, and, whenever he observed any

well-dressed women, pulled his hat off and bowed to them. At dinner he conversed as usual, was inquisitive about the kinds of fish produced on the coast of England, and ate part of a turbot that was at table, with much relish.' He spoke quite openly of the cross-channel activities of the local seafaring community. 'They are generally smugglers as well as fishermen; at one time a great many of them were in my pay, for the purpose of obtaining intelligence, bringing money over to France, and assisting prisoners of war to escape.'

On the 26th Captain Maitland received orders to proceed to Plymouth Sound, which the Admiralty considered more secure than Tor Bay. Napoleon's companions were disappointed by the move westward because they had hoped the Emperor would be invited for talks in London; he himself made no comment.

That same afternoon the *Bellerophon* rounded Start Point and sailed into Plymouth Sound. Napoleon remained on deck through most of the voyage, enjoying the beauties of the Devon coastline, as the hills and tors of Dartmoor shimmered in the distance. He chatted with Captain Maitland while they were approaching Plymouth and showed great interest in the breakwater, then being built. No sooner had they anchored than boats began to gather. Over the next week or so he became the most exciting tourist attraction the county can ever have known. Each day thousands of small vessels, loaded and overloaded with the curious, the critical, the nosey and the admiring, entered the Sound from far and wide, making for *Bellerophon*. Navy cutters patrolled the waters to stop people boarding the frigate, and the *Liffey* and *Eurotas* anchored on either side. At night they even fired across the bows of sightseeing craft until Napoleon voiced his concern. 'It worries and grieves me,' he told Captain Maitland. 'I should be obliged if you could put a stop to it.' Maitland did as he was bid.

So strictly were orders obeyed that even the Captain's wife was turned back and could not visit her husband.

Napoleon thought it very hard. When she was pointed out to him, he bowed in the direction of her boat, telling Maitland she was even prettier than her portrait. He arranged for some of his French wine to be sent to her, but the bottles were later confiscated by Customs officials. He was very struck by the beauty of the English women that he saw, and commented on how well they dressed.

After a few days, some of *Bellerophon*'s sailors, caught up in the drama of it all, furnished themselves with a blackboard and chalks, by which means they kept the public informed of their imperial passenger's movements. News flashes were displayed such as 'At Breakfast', 'In His Cabin', 'Dictating to His Officers', 'Coming on Deck' and 'At Dinner'. These communiqués were greeted with rapt attention, kindling animated discussion. In fact, he rarely appeared on deck until about five in the afternoon, spending much of his time reading, dozing or pacing up and down the Great Cabin. One book that particularly absorbed him was a life of George Washington — he may still have cherished hopes of being allowed to settle in America.

However, at eleven in the morning of 31st July he received a visit from the Lord High Admiral, Viscount Keith, who informed him that his future had been decided: he was to be confined for the rest of his life to Saint Helena; he could take three officers, a doctor and twelve servants. Napoleon was downcast, but remained calm.

The same afternoon, a sightseer went out from Torpoint and wrote to a friend saying so many boats were crowded round the *Bellerophon* that 'the sea appeared literally like dry land.' At about half past six Napoleon came on deck.

'He stood uncovered in full dress, on the step of the gangway, his Marshals in a compact circle behind him, certainly a most majestic figure. He was dressed in blue coat, red cuffs, white breeches and white silk stockings, his hat in one hand, his glass in the other.'

79

The possibilities of so picturesque and historic a scene were not lost on a 21 year old Plymouth painter, Charles Eastlake. He rowed out to the *Bellerophon* each afternoon, filling his sketchbooks with drawings during the few minutes that the great man stood on deck. With his eagle eye Napoleon was soon able to spot the artist among the crowds and held a characteristic pose for him on repeated occasions. In addition, he arranged for a uniform and some of his decorations to be delivered to Eastlake's studio, so that the young man could faithfully reproduce every detail of his appearance. The completed canvas, in oils, measuring eight and a half ft by six, was later viewed by Captain Maitland and some of Napoleon's officers, all of whom found it so remarkable that they signed documents testifying to the extraordinary likeness achieved. The painting attracted such interest that a London gallery asked to display it. After creating a furore in the capital, it was exhibited in a number of provincial cities and purchased by a syndicate of five Plymouth businessmen. It now hangs in the National Maritime Museum at Greenwich. Eastlake became famous, and since his proceeds amounted to the very substantial sum of £1,000, he was able to spend the next 14 years travelling abroad, greatly increasing his knowledge and capabilities. He declined the art professorship at London University when it opened in 1833, but became Plymouth's only-ever President of the Royal Academy in 1850 and Director of the National Gallery in 1855.

Eastlake's distinguished career could be said to spring from the success of this portrait. What a shame that its obliging subject was never to see it! However, his sojourn in Plymouth waters was fast drawing to a close. The Prime Minister, Lord Liverpool, was becoming ever more anxious about Napoleon's burgeoning popularity: the wicked ogre of fable had turned into Prince Charming. Officers and sailors on the *Bellerophon* were now his open admirers; they even performed a play for his amusement. Crowds grew thicker every day. 'A little longer, and he will have all the nation for him,' declared Viscount Keith. 'Damn the fellow! If he obtained an interview with His Royal Highness, in half an hour they would be the best friends in England.' Lord Liverpool confessed to his Foreign Secretary Lord Castlereagh on 3rd August, 'Bonaparte is giving us great trouble at Plymouth,' so he ordered the *Bellerophon* to put to sea. Captain Maitland weighed anchor on the following day and cruised a few miles east of Start Bay, waiting to meet the *Northumberland*, which was being hastily fitted out at Portsmouth to take Napoleon to Saint Helena.

In very heavy weather at nine o'clock on the morning of 7th August the *Northumberland* hove into view, escorted by two frigates bristling with troops. Viscount Keith came on board to supervise the ex-Emperor's embarkation and, against regulations, permitted him to continue wearing his sword. Napoleon took leave of those members of his staff who would not be accompanying him to Saint Helena. Most of them were weeping; they kissed his hands, and he embraced them. He bade farewell to Captain Maitland, calling him a man of honour and thanking him for their brief friendship. He tried to make him accept a snuffbox, but the Englishman, already under suspicion for his loyalties, had to decline. Then, despite being previously censured for it, Captain Maitland again treated him as royalty by mustering the entire crew, bareheaded, on deck. He had the guard present arms and the drums roll as Napoleon descended to the boat that would take him across to his new ship.

The *Northumberland* headed westward, then cruised outside Plymouth Sound in rough seas until joined on 9th August by eight further escort vessels and two freighters carrying provisions. This fleet then set sail for Saint Helena. During the nine week voyage Napoleon celebrated his 46th birthday and was toasted by the English officers. He died in Saint Helena six years later.

81

A Deadly Affair

A YOUNG woman forced to marry a man against all her own inclinations was a common occurrence in Elizabethan England. Marriages were often arranged by parents or guardians to enhance family fortunes or prestige, and daughters were just chattels to be profitably bestowed. Obedience from the prospective bride was expected — after all, what choice did she have? One Devonshire lass, Eulalia Glanville, finding herself in this hateful situation, wed to a disgusting old man who treated her like a servant, eventually decided she did have a choice — she had him murdered.

He was a goldsmith named Page, who lived in a tall gabled house in Woolster Street, Plymouth, one of the many narrow lanes that edged Sutton Pool. His canny trading had earned him a tidy fortune but, being a mean obnoxious fellow, he was determined that none of his relatives should inherit his wealth. He resolved to wreck their foolish expectations by marrying a young submissive wife who would promptly, dutifully, produce an heir for him. His lascivious eye fell on Eulalia, the daughter of a Tavistock merchant, Nicolas Glanville.

Eulalia, blissfully unaware of his intentions, was enjoying her first romance. Her suitor was a handsome lieutenant on a man-of-war, George Strangwidge, and they planned to marry once his naval duties were over. Her parents had given their approval and she thought she was the happiest girl in the world. But, as soon as the rich goldsmith expressed an interest in her, Nicolas Glanville sternly forbade her to think any further of her dashing lover.

Dazed with shock, she heard of her father's ambitious plans for her as the wife of old Page. Nauseated at the prospect, Eulalia hurriedly wrote a tear-drenched letter to George, begging him to rescue her from such a cruel fate. Days and weeks went by, but no answer was received. More appeals were sent, while she stood out against relentless parental pressure. No response came from him, and she was at last persuaded to believe that he had abandoned her. In great distress, she listlessly allowed herself to become Mrs Page.

Triumphantly, the bridegroom returned with his wife to Plymouth and installed her in his house. He reduced his household expenses by making Eulalia do the work of a maidservant. The dreary months wore on as the poor girl grew ever more miserable. Then, out of the blue one day, George appeared at her door. Tears and embraces were exchanged as the young man explained how he had written to her imploring her to resist the marriage until he could come to her, and how devastated he had been to discover that she had been forced to obey her father. They realised, with overwhelming dismay, that his letters had been intercepted by her parents to prevent their romance continuing. As they bewailed their separation, an insistent idea kept popping into Eulalia's head — if only the old fool would die! It was but a short step to the foolhardy plan to help him on his way.

Within a little while, the lovers had enlisted some help. A manservant, Robert Prideaux, was drawn into the conspiracy by a promise of money, as was Tom Stone, a friend of George Strangwidge. Eulalia, having made the decision to murder her husband, was in a hurry to get it over with. On a freezing night in February 1591, she could wait no longer. She gathered her killers, Prideaux and Stone, and led them to the unsuspecting victim's bedchamber. One moment old Page was snoring peacefully under his blankets and the next he was thrashing around, kicking and scratching, frantically gasping for air as iron-hard fingers slowly throttled him.

After a fearful struggle, the goldsmith succumbed and lay lifeless on a tangled heap of bedclothes.

Just then a shower of small stones thudded against the window. Eulalia quickly opened it to find her lover gazing anxiously upward.

'For God's sake stay your hand!' he pleaded, overcome with self-loathing at plotting cold-blooded murder.

''Tis too late, the deed is done,' Eulalia coolly replied.

Unfortunately for the couple, this incriminating exchange was overheard by Page's neighbour, disturbed by the noise. When, next morning, the news leaked out that the old man had died suddenly during the night, the neighbour reported the conversation to the Mayor of Plymouth, who ordered an immediate investigation. A hurried attempt by the murderers to get Page into his coffin and out of sight was just too late. When the body was examined it was obvious that death was not due to natural causes — livid fingermarks around the corpse's throat, plus multiple bruises and scratches on the body, were plainly visible.

Strangwidge, Prideaux, Stone and Eulalia were arrested on the spot and committed for trial at Barnstaple. They would have been taken to Exeter Gaol, but plague was rife there, and with the memory of the Black Assize of 1586, when the judge, eight justices and the entire jury save one died of gaol fever, it was thought safer to move the Assizes of March 1591 to the clearer air of Barnstaple.

The outcome of the trial was never in doubt. All four were found guilty and condemned to death. Eulalia showed no signs of remorse. She stoutly declared that she would rather die with her lover than to have continued her forlorn existence with old Page. The gibbet was erected on the castle green so that the execution could be witnessed by the townsfolk. The three men were brought out together and, with very little fuss, dispatched to the hereafter. Their bodies danced gently in the breeze for a while, then were cut down and buried.

For Eulalia there was no burial. There was nothing left to bury. A wife convicted of killing her husband was guilty not just of murder but of petty treason. The punishment for this crime was far more ferocious than mere hanging. Eulalia was burned alive.

One of the lawyers who had defended her at Barnstaple was her uncle, John Glanville, later to become an eminent judge. He stood beside his niece when her dreadful sentence was pronounced, and a little later witnessed her agonising death. It is said that he never smiled again.

Fairs, Feasts, Fun and Frolics

'Tom Pearce, Tom Pearce, lend me your grey mare,
All along, down along, out along lee,
For I want for to go to Widecombe Fair,
Wi' Bill Brewer, Jan Stewer, Peter Gurney, Peter Davy,
Dan'l Whiddon, Harry Hawk, and old Uncle Tom Cobley
and all,
Old Uncle Tom Cobley and all.'

EVERYBODY has heard of Widecombe Fair. It is the most famous fair in England, thanks entirely to the old song which has been popular for more than a hundred years. The Devonshire Regiment adopted the tune as their regimental quick march, so it has been played all over the world. But what do we know about the fair itself? In its early days it was just a pony and cattle fair, held every September, where the animals which had grazed Dartmoor all summer were sold. After the business deals were concluded there was, naturally, time for gossip and junketing. Tom Cobley and his seven companions journeyed 14 miles across the moor from their home village of Spreyton to enjoy the fun. Yes, they really did exist! Tom Cobley died around 1794 and was buried in the churchyard of St Michael's, Spreyton, in an unmarked grave near the south porch. The village inn is called after him. Of course, a major part of the modern Widecombe

Fair festivities includes a re-enactment of the famous ride on Tom Pearce's poor old horse.

Many of Devon's fairs and festivals feature some pretty large-scale eating and drinking. A truly fantastic example of this centres on the Paignton Pudding, a sort of monstrous dumpling, which used to be made during the June Charter Fair for the townsfolk to eat. Thomas Westcote wrote about it in 1630.

'Somewhat I must tell you of the huge and costly white-pot there made of late; some term it a bag pudding. In former ages it was an annual action, and of that greatness that is incredible to the hearer; but thence it hath the addition of white-pot, and called Paignton White-pot.'

By the end of the 17th century the 'annual action' had dwindled to an occasional effort to commemorate some great event. We know that the pudding was made again in 1809 and that it consisted of 400 pounds of flour, 170 pounds of beef suet, 140 pounds of raisins and 240 eggs. This jumbo dessert was boiled in a brewer's copper for four days before being deemed edible. It was loaded onto a decorated cart pulled by eight oxen and paraded through the streets, after which it was distributed among the spectators, who complained bitterly that it was rock hard on the outside and soggy in the middle.

After such disappointing eating, the pudding was not attempted again until August 1859, when the arrival of the railway in Paignton called for a bumper celebration. A new recipe was concocted, one which would ensure an unforgettable Paignton Pudding. The ingredients were 573 pounds of flour, 191 pounds of bread, 573 pounds of dried fruit, 382 pounds of suet, 320 lemons, 144 nutmegs, 95 pounds of sugar, 720 pints of milk and hundreds of eggs. It was baked in sections and then assembled like a pyramid. The circumference at the base was over 13 ft.

The gargantuan plum pudding, weighing more than a ton, was drawn through the town on a wagon pulled by 25 horses. Behind the wagon walked the railway navvies, who were to be honoured guests at the feast, waving and shouting cheerily to the vast numbers of onlookers lining the route. All went according to plan until the time came for the carving of the pudding, when there was a sudden undignified scramble to grab a slice from guests and spectators alike. Paignton's five policemen waded into the crush to try and restore some semblance of order to the proceedings, but it was quite hopeless. The unhappy carvers, frightened by the press of bodies surrounding them, began to throw great lumps of pudding into the crowd to fend them off. Within a remarkably short space of time, the whole colossal structure had vanished. Not a crumb remained.

It is hardly surprising that no-one could face the thought of Paignton Pudding for some years after the near-riot of 1859. Mr George Hill baked one in 1871, which he paraded in a cart pulled by six donkeys, but it was of a more manageable size and there was no repetition of unruly behaviour.

At just about the same time that Mr Hill was toiling over his pudding, another custom associated with vigorous appetites was making its first appearance in the village of Branscombe, between Seaton and Sidmouth. It began when some naughty little boys stole a very large apple pie which they cut into slices and sold for pocket money. From this reprehensible inauguration grew the Branscombe Apple Pie Fair, an annual jollification held in September. Numbers of huge apple pies, made by the local baker, are displayed on a wagon decked with autumn flowers and foliage and drawn through the village, before being cut up and shared among the spectators, without any of the disorderliness exhibited in Paignton.

A feast with a more sinister history, a relic of pre-Christian days when Spring fertility rites and animal sacrifice in honour of the old gods were a vital part of pastoral life, is the Ram Fair at Kingsteignton, near Newton Abbot. Here, a ram lamb is killed, decorated with flowers and ribbons and paraded round the town before being roasted, sliced and eaten. Two Dartmoor villages, Buckland-in-the-Moor and Holne, used to celebrate Midsummer Day and May Day (the time of the Celtic Fire Festival of Beltane) by sacrificing a ram lamb. He would be caught by the young men of the village, tied to a standing stone and his throat cut. The men would sprinkle themselves with warm blood before roasting the lamb whole, wool and all. Everyone, young or old, male or female, was anxious for a slice of roasted ram, since it was believed to confer luck for the year on the eater.

At Ashburton, the drink rather than the food is the highlight of its fair. This ancient town, on the very edge of Dartmoor, still clings to its Saxon heritage by appointing a Portreeve instead of a Mayor, whose duties have included choosing various officials at the annual Court Leet in November to be bread-weighers, pig-drivers, or ale-tasters. The ale-taster was responsible for ensuring that the local brew was of the right strength. He would enter an inn, demand a mug of ale and pour it on a wooden bench. He would then plonk himself in the puddle for half an hour. If sugar had been added to the ale, his trousers would be stuck to the bench! He had to visit each of the ten public houses in Ashburton and sample the beer. If it was found adequate, the landlord was presented with an evergreen sprig to display on his front door. In recent times, the Ale Tasting Ceremony has been a part of the St Lawrence Fair merrymaking.

But, unfortunately, not all of Devon's fairs could always be relied on to provide liberal quantities of their particular speciality, as the 22 year old John Keats discovered after a three-mile hike along the coast from Teignmouth to Dawlish Fair on Easter Monday, 23rd March 1818. He was so disappointed with the delicacies on offer that, when he

got home, he dashed down his opinion of the outing in a
letter to his friend James Rice.

'Over the Hill and over the Dale,
And over the bourne to Dawlish —
Where Gingerbread Wives have a scanty sale,
And Gingerbread nuts are smallish.'

Of Puffins
and Pirates

WHEN somebody mentions Lundy, do you think of puffins? Well, so, too, did the Vikings, for Lundy means Puffin Island in Old Norse. Puffins have lived on Lundy for centuries, breeding in colonies on the steep and rocky coast. After years of decline, their numbers are again increasing. They share their windswept home with thousands of other birds — razorbills, guillemots, cormorants, oystercatchers, gulls, lapwings and kittiwakes all find sanctuary here. Passing high fliers grateful for a stopover include golden plovers, redshanks, turtle doves and hoopoes. Over 400 varieties of birds have been spotted on the island, including the first sighting in Britain of an American robin and a Baltimore oriole.

But not all Lundy's residents and visitors have been such enchanting birds of passage. The island's position in the Bristol Channel 14 miles north-west of Hartland Point, and its air of bleak impregnability made it a sanctuary for birds of a different feather — seaborne desperadoes whose aim in life was to plunder the shipping plying up and down the Bristol Channel. In short, it was a pirate's paradise.

The first recorded pirate king of Lundy was William de Marisco, a 13th century disgraced nobleman, whose family had owned the island for a hundred years. He had once possessed large estates in the West Country and Ireland before falling foul of Henry III, who confiscated them. In desperation William fled to Lundy, his last stronghold, where for the next seven years he reigned supreme. From his island fortress, he made devastating raids on merchant ships not only in the Bristol Channel but off the coasts of Scotland and Ireland. He probably could have ruled as long as he wished, but his gnawing resentment against his monarch eventually got the better of him and he resolved to take his revenge. He instructed one of his knights to infiltrate the royal court and assassinate the king. The attempt failed, but so incensed Henry that, having turned a blind eye to William's piratical activities, he now determined to put an end to him. He dispatched to Devon a unit of his best soldiers under the command of William Bardolph, a leader noted for bravery and daring. One misty morning towards the end of May 1242 they embarked from Bideford and landed at the one place where they might be able to scale the cliffs unobserved.

After successfully negotiating the slippery, sometimes perpendicular, rockface, they reached the top, only to be confronted by what they least expected — a sentry. But by a stroke of good fortune he proved to be a man detained on Lundy against his will, and Bardolph was able to persuade him to guide them to William's headquarters. The pirate king and most of his followers, caught unawares, nevertheless provided stout resistance, but were finally overpowered and captured. They were taken first to Bristol, then to the Tower of London. William was found guilty of high treason and murder. On 25th July 1242 he was dragged by horse to the gibbet, where he was hanged, disembowelled and quartered, the quarters being put on display in various towns around London.

Many other pirates over the years used Lundy as a base, including Algerian raiders on slaving expeditions round the south-west coast. But the most ineffectual pirate leader of all time must be Thomas Salkeld. He declared himself King of Lundy in 1610, captured one or two nondescript vessels and enslaved the occupants. After a short while the 'slaves' decided they had had enough of King Thomas, planned a revolt and overthrew the unhappy monarch, who fled in terror and was never seen again.

Another villain connected with Lundy who has gone into the history books is Sir Lewis 'Judas' Stukeley, originally from Affeton Castle near Witheridge in North Devon. A kinsman of Sir Walter Raleigh, he became Vice-Admiral of Devon. James I ordered him to arrest Raleigh when the great hero returned empty-handed to Plymouth in 1618 after his fruitless quest for the golden city of El Dorado. Stukeley did as he was bid in the simple time-honoured way — betrayal, hence his nickname. Worming his way into Raleigh's confidence, he learnt of his planned escape to France. Without a moment's hesitation, he had his illustrious relative seized just as Sir Walter was about to board ship at Greenwich. Shocked at Stukeley's treachery, Raleigh warned him, 'Sir Lewis, these actions will not turn out to your credit.'

His words, hinting at future ignominy, were prophetic. Soon after Stukeley had received a £500 pay-off from King James for his services, he was found guilty of clipping gold coins and, though spared the death penalty, had to leave London and return to his Affeton estate. Here he was treated with repugnance not only by neighbours and former friends, but even by his servants and retainers. In despair he persuaded Lundy's owner Sir Barnard Grenville, a distant relative, to let him live in isolation at Marisco Castle. He shut himself up in the lonely tower, where within a short time he went raving mad, tormented by the roaring sea, screeching wind and jabbering birds. He died a year later, in 1620, and was buried at South Molton, near Barnstaple, for Affeton would not have him.

Only a few hundred yards from Marisco Castle is Benson's Cave, named after the most resourceful of all Lundy's malefactors, William Benson, born in 1707 at Northam, between Bideford and Appledore. Living at Knapp House, now the centre of a Northam holiday complex, he inherited wealth and became the most successful merchant on the North Devon coast. Described as 'the life and support of the commercial enterprise of Appledore and Bideford', he was elected a Sheriff of Devon in 1746 and MP for Barnstaple in 1747. He cultivated friendships in high places and won a valuable government contract for shipping convicts to Virginia and Maryland. During 1748 he obtained the lease of Lundy from Lord Gower at a rental of £60 a year.

The island had been uninhabited and neglected for three decades, its few buildings disintegrating, the land uncultivated. Amid general surprise Benson now began to revive and restore it, incurring what appeared to be wasted expense, since the place gave little sign of imminent productivity. However, he also excavated vast caves and used them like bonded warehouses, storing great quantities of imported merchandise, particularly tobacco, which would otherwise have attracted heavy duties. As for ferrying convicts across the Atlantic, he merely landed them at Lundy and employed them under guard in repairs, construction, drainage and farming; several miles of their walls are still standing today. 'Sending convicts to Lundy is the same as sending them to America,' he told a friend. 'It matters not where it is, so long as they are out of the country.' The authorities must have agreed, for they turned a blind eye to this limited form of transportation.

They were not so indulgent about his smuggling operations, for within two years of his leasing Lundy he received his first financial penalties, amounting to £900. These were followed by more substantial fines which by 1751 totalled over £8,000, reinforced by lightning raids and confiscations. Such crippling reversals completely undermined Benson's economic position, and the collapse was total when his Knapp House estate was impounded. At this point he planned the crime that proved his undoing.

He heavily insured an almost unseaworthy old brigantine supposedly bound for Maryland with convicts from Exeter and a valuable cargo of pewter, linen and salt.

This worm-eaten tub, the *Nightingale*, lumbered out of Bideford on 27th July 1752, collected the 16 convicts at Barnstaple and made for Lundy, where most of the cargo was unloaded. The captain, John Lancey, then took the ship 50 miles westward and, finding another vessel nearby, the *Charming Nancy* from Philadelphia, ordered wads of tarred oakum to be ignited in the hold. When the American skipper, Captain Nicholson, saw smoke billowing from the *Nightingale*, he altered course and rescued those on board. He offered to help extinguish the fire, but Lancey warned him of gunpowder in the cargo.

After abandoning the stricken ship and being brought safely ashore at Milford Haven, Lancey hired a boat, returned to Bideford and locked the convicts in a barn. He reported his satisfactory progress to Benson. So far, so good, with an impeccable witness to the catastrophe. But James Bather, the sailor who lit the fire, was soon into a Barnstaple snug with his £50 bounty. Lancey should have locked him in the barn with the convicts, for under the influence of alcohol he babbled of the adventure. Somebody sent for Benson's business rival Matthew Reeder, who gently coaxed the whole sorry tale from the merry mariner. Once in possession of all the facts, Reeder informed Benson's insurance company. Shortly afterwards Lancey was arrested together with three other members of the crew. They were eventually arraigned before the Court of Admiralty at the Old Bailey, when Lancey was found guilty of burning the *Nightingale* with intent to defraud. He was condemned to death and hanged at Wapping in June 1754.

In the nick of time Benson escaped to Portugal and, against all odds, managed to build a rewarding new career. He became one of the leading traders in Oporto, where he died at the age of 64 in 1772. In the history of Lundy he was as remarkable a rare bird as the Baltimore oriole — though somewhat less familiar with Maryland!

Entertaining
Dr Johnson

'WHEN a man is tired of London, he is tired of life,' said
the oft-quoted Samuel Johnson. But the great
author was always happy to quit London for a month or
two if a friend offered him an interesting holiday. He was
an enthusiastic traveller, and we know about many of his
journeys from James Boswell. However, one trip has never
received much prominence, mainly because it took place
the year before Johnson and Boswell met. In his life of
Johnson, Boswell mentions it briefly among the events of
1762. 'This year his friend Sir Joshua Reynolds paid a visit
of some weeks to his native county, Devonshire, in which he
was accompanied by Johnson, who was much pleased with
this jaunt.'

Luckily, Reynolds' notebook for 1762 still exists and is
kept at the Royal Academy of Arts, whose President he
became in 1768. From it we learn that the painter and
writer set out from London by coach at two in the
afternoon on Monday 16th August. Because of his
short-sightedness, Johnson derived little pleasure from
gazing at the passing scene. Instead, he would often read a
favourite Latin author, until some strand of conversation
from his fellow passengers prompted his participation, at
which he would pour forth his knowledge and eloquence
'in a full stream, to the delight and astonishment of his
auditors.' The subject was unpredictable; on one occasion
he spoke lengthily and spellbindingly on the digestive
problems of dogs.

Travelling via Winchester, Salisbury, Wilton, Blandford Forum, Dorchester and Bridport, they reached Axminster on Saturday 21st August. Then, passing through Exeter, they made their way to Great Torrington, where two of Sir Joshua's sisters lived. On Thursday 26th August they called on his sister Mary, whose fine house in New Street is still standing. She was married to John Palmer, who became mayor of Torrington three times. Yet another of Reynolds' sisters, Frances, was staying with them at the time, so Johnson had an agreeable supply of feminine company, which invariably put him in a good mood. In good appetite, too — when Mary asked him if he liked pancakes, he answered, 'Yes, madam, but I never get enough of them,' and at dinner packed away 13, displaying digestive powers that a dog might envy.

On one of his three days at Torrington, Frances took him out to Weare Giffard and showed him a monument placed by a widowed mother over the grave of her only child. She had to cut short her sad narrative of explanation when Johnson burst into tears. At Langtree he was entertained by the Rev Thomas Morrison, one of whose poems he later got published in London.

They left on the 28th and, after spending the night at Okehampton, reached Plymouth the following evening, where they stopped for three weeks with Sir Joshua's childhood friend Dr John Mudge in St Nicholas Yard. Their host was not only a physician but a leading mathematician and pioneer in the development of the astronomical telescope. Among several scientifically gifted friends whom he introduced to Johnson was William Cookworthy, originator of the first British process for manufacturing true porcelain. In 1759, concerned by the number of Plymouth seamen dying of scurvy, Cookworthy identified the anti-scorbutic properties of fresh fruit and vegetables and recommended them with sauerkraut for all long voyages. Noting also the gradual deterioration of drinking water stored in ships, he invented a method of distilling sea water that could be carried out under sail. In a gathering of Dr Mudge's learned friends Johnson was asked somewhat fancifully if he was a botanist. 'No, sir, I am not a botanist,' he replied and added, alluding to his shortsightedness, 'Should I wish to become a botanist, I must first turn myself into a reptile.'

During their time in Plymouth, Johnson and Reynolds visited the homes of various eminent Devonians, including local MPs. They were guests of the Veales at Coffleet, between Combe and Brixton, and of the Parkers at Saltram House. They stayed overnight with the Bastards at Kitley Court, near Yealmpton. Here 60 years later Sarah Martin, a relative of the Bastards, wrote the nursery rhyme *Old Mother Hubbard*, which is believed to be based on the family's housekeeper. Perhaps this storybook character, before becoming even Young Mother Hubbard, was in service at Kitley Court and waited on the great Dr Johnson.

One of the highlights of their holiday was a trip to see John Smeaton's recently completed Eddystone Lighthouse, deemed a wonder of the age. Johnson's interest would have been quickened by Dr Mudge, a close friend of Smeaton, and by Cookworthy, with whom the engineer lodged during the building's three year construction. Learning of Johnson's desire to visit the lighthouse, the Commissioner of Plymouth Dockyard, Sir Frederick Rogers, arranged for a yacht to take him and Reynolds there on 9th September. Unfortunately, rough seas prevented them from landing and being given a guided tour. At around this time Johnson conceived a hatred for the rapidly developing town of Devonport. He viewed it from Mount Edgcumbe and from the yacht, and he found it an eyesore. 'I am a Plymouth man!' he proclaimed.

He seems to have enjoyed himself greatly in Plymouth, astonishing the natives with prodigious powers of eating and drinking. He once described himself as 'a hardened and shameless tea-drinker . . . whose kettle has scarcely time to cool; who with tea amuses the evening, with tea solaces the midnight, and with tea welcomes the morning.' At the home of Dr Mudge's father, the distinguished vicar of St Andrew's, Zachariah Mudge, he drank 17 cups in a row. His hostess grew a little vexed to see her precious stock of tea laid waste, but, after all, she should have remembered she was providing refreshment for the man who wrote

'Yet hear, alas! this mournful truth,
Nor hear it with a frown —
Thou canst not make the tea so fast
As I can gulp it down.'

His drinking did not stop at tea. One evening after dinner he dispatched three bottles of wine, which affected his speech as never before, so that he could not articulate a particular word at the first three attempts. He succeeded on his fourth try, and prudently retired to bed. At another time he put away such quantities of new cider, together with vast dollops of clotted cream and fresh honey, that his host found himself 'much embarrassed between his anxious regard for the Doctor's health and his fear of breaking through the rules of politeness by giving him a hint on the subject.' He need not have worried, for Johnson's formidable constitution triumphantly survived the onslaught. Indeed, he quickly acquired in Plymouth circles the same renown as a trencherman that he already held as a writer, and hostesses vied with each other in producing bigger and better feasts for his delectation. However, some of these ladies were less observant or subtle than others in their ministrations. It was usually clear when the Doctor had taken enough tea: he would turn his cup upside down in the saucer, a practice often followed in London teahouses. But with food, of which there was a considerably varied spread, you could not always be certain whether he had finished, and you had to be careful not to press him. One hostess unfortunately rather overdid it. Johnson suddenly pushed back his chair, rose to his feet and, clutching his butter-knife like a dagger, thundered, 'I vow to God I cannot eat a bit more!' which apparently struck terror into the hearts of several guests present.

But most of the time he was in a genial, light-hearted mood, feeling very much at home in the bustling maritime city. During one visit his hostess drew his attention to page 293 of his *Dictionary* and asked him how he came to define 'pastern' as the knee of a horse. 'Ignorance, madam, pure ignorance,' he replied. That same afternoon a young woman boasted she could run faster than anybody else. 'Madam, you cannot outrun me,' said Johnson, accepting her challenge. They had a race, which he lost. Then he kicked off his ill-fitting shoes, and they had another race, which he won by quite a distance. Leading her by the hand, he returned to the teatable looking extremely pleased with himself.

On 22nd September, four days after Johnson's 53rd birthday, the two holidaymakers took their leave of Dr and Mrs Mudge and went to Reynolds' birthplace, Plympton, where he was later elected mayor in honour of his achievements. They reached Exeter by the next evening and arrived in London on the 26th. Thus ended the Doctor's sole trip deep into the West Country.

Two months later Mrs Mudge gave birth to a son, William, who rose to be a major-general. He had a good start in life: his godfather was Samuel Johnson.

The
Bideford Witches

A VISITOR to the North Devon town of Bideford in the
1680s would have received a most favourable first
impression. A thriving market town and port, Bideford
was trading vigorously with the American colonies and its
quay was crowded with ships large and small. Cotton and
woollen goods were among the most important exports,
while tobacco was imported in greater quantities than to
any other port in England. Wealthy and successful
merchants and mariners lived in substantial houses in
Bridgeland Street, just off the quay. The zealous
Puritanism of the best families added to the general
atmosphere of prosperity. But a more penetrating look by
our traveller would have revealed a very different and
rather nastier picture.

In common with most English towns of that period,
Bideford was a dirty smelly place. In 1673 its councillors
complained of the 'noisome and stinking dunghills and
other filth which too frequently has been cast out in
hedges, in several streets and on the quay of the town, and
suffered to lie long there' and of the 'hogs and swines
permitted to run up and down the town.' Life for the mass
of ignorant poor folk was usually brief and unpleasant.
Amusements were few, consisting mainly of drunken
brawling in illegal boozing dens or pelting unwilling
residents in the stocks.

Much more exciting was the popular sport of

witch-hunting, undertaken with the encouragement of religious fanatics who truly believed that demented old women, or voluptuous young ones, habitually consorted with Satan. Witchcraft had been a capital crime since 1542 and many thousands of women were burned, hanged, drowned or otherwise murdered in the name of the law. Most remain anonymous, but the trial of three unfortunates from Bideford in 1682 caused such a stir that it prompted the publication of a ballad and a broadsheet in London, ensuring a lasting memorial to the women known as the Bideford Witches

They lived in a thatched cottage in Higher Gunstone Lane — Temperance Lloyd, Susanna Edwards and Mary Trembles. Temperance, an elderly dame whose name did not suit her inclinations, had been accused of witchcraft on two previous occasions but released for lack of evidence. On 26th July 1682 she was arrested for the third time on a warrant signed by Thomas Gift, the Mayor of Bideford, and Alderman John Davie. In prison, confused and alone, old Temperance babbled distractedly of her two companions. Within a very short time, charges of witchcraft had been levelled against them and they joined her in custody.

Dragged before the magistrates, the women were confronted by their accusers. Dorcas Coleman, wife of a Bideford seaman, claimed that since August 1680 she had been tormented with stabbing pains in her stomach, arms and heart. Dr Beare had been summoned to cure her affliction but he had immediately declared that it was quite beyond his power to help as she was obviously bewitched. Soon afterwards, Susanna Edwards visited her in her bedchamber and stood motionless, staring at her. Dorcas was then beset by such agony that she could neither speak nor see. She was quite certain that Susanna was indeed a witch.

The next woman, Grace Thomas, told a similar tale of violent pricking pains all over her body, which were particularly bad in her head and feet. She had suffered continuously for six months during 1680 then had gradually improved, although she still found it difficult to sleep. On meeting Temperance Lloyd in the street one day, she was taken aback at the old crone's peculiar concern for her health. That very night, and from then on, the torture had increased so that her bed felt like a rack. Just before the arrest of Temperance the pangs had become so fierce that she imagined her flesh was being torn from her head and limbs by devilish fingers, but as soon as the witch was locked up Grace started to recover.

As the evidence began to mount up against Temperance, Grace Thomas seized her advantage and produced a witness — her landlady Elizabeth Eastchurch. When Grace had complained of stinging pains in her knee, Elizabeth had carefully examined it and discovered nine tiny puncture holes. She accosted Temperance outside her cottage and demanded to know whether she had made a wax image of her victim which she stuck with pins. Naturally the old woman denied anything of the sort, but eventually admitted owning a small piece of leather with pinholes in it.

The next witness was Anne Wakely, who had examined the prisoner to ascertain if she bore any strange marks on her body which might prove she was a witch. She had discovered two little strips of flesh, each about an inch long, placed side by side, which she identified as secret teats for the Devil to suckle from. Temperance was certainly a witch — there was no doubt about it.

After this bizarre evidence had been given, Temperance was questioned by the magistrates. Whether from fear or bravado, or a lunatic desire to astound her accusers, she began to babble of her dealings with Satan. She bragged of meeting him near her home two years previously. She described him as a 'Black Man' about two ft high with huge staring eyes and a mouth like a toad. She swore that he had suckled from her secret teats while she knelt down in the road. She insisted that he had made them both invisible so that they could torment Grace Thomas, pinching and pricking her almost to death.

Susanna's testimony was just as nonsensical as her companion's. She too jabbered of a little 'Black Man', alleging that he not only suckled from her, he also had carnal knowledge of her body. Seemingly determined to outdo Temperance in wickedness, she spoke of her powers of invisibility, and how she and the Devil had tortured Dorcas Coleman and Grace Barnes by pinching and pricking. Hearing this declaration, another woman was encouraged to come forward and assert that her husband had been bewitched by Susanna, causing him to caper about the room like a madman, quivering and foaming at the mouth before falling unconscious to the floor, lying like a dead man for nearly an hour.

The confession of the third 'witch', Mary Trembles, was truly pathetic. She could only stammer that she might once have seen the Devil disguised as a lion. Unfortunately for her, she was completely dominated by Susanna Edwards and would do or say whatever the older woman decided.

When all the evidence had been heard against the trio, it was agreed that they should be taken to the church to be tested by the Rector, Mr Ogilby. Temperance was ordered to recite the Lord's Prayer, but the befuddled old dame was quite unable to manage it. Her failure proved to the assembled magistrates that all three women were witches. They were committed for trial at Exeter Assizes.

At Exeter Castle on 18th August 1682 the judge accepted all the testimony given at Bideford and sentenced the wretched prisoners to death for practising witchcraft and sorcery. Just one week later, on 25th August, they were taken to the place of execution — Heavitree Gallows, a mile outside the city. On the scaffold the women were interrogated in turn by a local priest. Poor Mary, quaking with terror, could only stutter a frantic and useless denial of any knowledge of the Devil. Temperance and Susanna, resigned to their doom, more calmly repudiated the charges against them. As Susanna prayed aloud, the hangman tightened the noose about her neck and launched her into space. Mary was next to die, but old Temperance endured one more inquisition from the Sheriff before the executioner finally ended her ordeal. The Bideford Witches were left dangling in a lifeless row.

The Treasure
of the
Madre de Dios

O N 7th September 1592 the biggest prize ever brought
back to England was steered into Dartmouth
Harbour. She was the massive seven-deck Portuguese
galleon *Madre de Dios*, captured a month earlier off the
Azores by a small privateering fleet whose sponsors
included Queen Elizabeth I and Sir Walter Raleigh. The
diminutive English men-of-war *Roebuck, Foresight, Dainty*
and *Golden Dragon* had harried the lofty treasure-ship for
several hours, sustaining many casualties in the process,
before some of the *Foresight's* crew eventually gained a
foothold. In the ferocious hand-to-hand fighting that
followed, as the Englishmen hurled themselves aboard, the
decks were awash with blood and strewn with corpses.
After a terrific battle the Portuguese crew, overwhelmed
by the savagery of the privateers, surrendered.

When the great ship was searched, she proved to be
carrying a stupendous cargo. There were 900 tons of East
Indian spices — cloves, pepper, nutmeg, ginger and
cinnamon; there were thousands of barrels of musk,
camphor and frankincense. Never before had anyone seen
so many bales of silks, satins, lace, damasks and taffetas, or
so many rolls of rare carpets and tapestries. But most
dazzling of all were chest upon chest of diamonds, rubies,

pearls, silver, gold, ivory, jade, porcelain and Oriental jewellery. In today's values, the entire cargo was worth more than £40 million.

Pillaging by the English seamen began at once, and by the time the galleon reached Dartmouth a considerable amount of her more portable booty was safely stowed away in bulging pockets and distended kitbags. Some of the privateer vessels astutely put into Plymouth ahead of the *Madre de Dios*'s arrival further along the coast, and their crews were off and away before the red-hot news hit town. But the docking of the treasure-ship did not have to be relayed by word of mouth to the people of Brixham, Paignton or Torquay. The south-westerly breezes that bore her into harbour also wafted on shore the pungent scents of the Orient, so that all the countryside guessed at her coming.

Now there was a headlong race to reach Dartmouth; across South Devon men set off on foot, horseback, or by boat. In no time, 2,000 hopefuls had arrived, including dozens of dealers and agents, whose ready cash encouraged the sailors to continue their plundering. A day later, goldsmiths, brokers and merchants from London and Bristol poured into town, offering even fatter inducements. Sailors paid for tankards of ale with lumps of amber and lured local beauties with pearl necklaces. One naval officer, ostensibly searching for stolen goods, bought 2,000 assorted precious stones from a looter for £130, then sold them at a handsome profit to a London jeweller.

Word soon reached the Government about the treasure of the *Madre de Dios*, and Lord Burghley sent his son Sir Robert Cecil to investigate. As he approached Exeter he soon became aware that every wayfarer who passed him seemed to have a bag 'that did smell of the prizes at Dartmouth.' On arriving at his destination, he was confronted by scenes unlike anything he had previously witnessed. 'There never was such spoil! Fouler ways, desperate ways, no more obstinate people did I ever meet with.' Lord Burghley had no alternative but to break the news to the Queen. As a chief investor in the privateering mission, Elizabeth was not amused. Much of the cargo that had been removed from the ship and was still daily being stolen belonged rightfully to her. She instructed Burghley to put an end to the mischief. He was unhappy with the idea of using force against men who, after all, had won a stunning naval engagement on England's behalf. Instead he asked the supreme national hero and Devon's greatest son, Sir Francis Drake, to go to Dartmouth and persuade the marauders to desist.

The man who had repulsed the Armada and circum-navigated the world immediately set off from his home — Buckland Abbey, near Tavistock. He spent hours with the privateers, assuring them that the *Madre de Dios* was not theirs to loot. But the sailors were first disappointed, and then annoyed, by his attitude, for here was someone whom they thought they were imitating, even if on a small scale. It was well known that he had condoned pillaging by the *Golden Hind*'s seamen on at least 20 occasions. So the men at Dartmouth flatly refused to listen to him, and he had to report a singular lack of success to the Council.

Lord Burghley racked his brains for another messenger to send to quell the recalcitrant mariners, since the matter was now becoming urgent. Sir John Hawkins, Treasurer and Controller of the Navy, suggested there was an 'especial man', another Devonian, who could 'bring this to some good effect.' The only snag was that the 'especial man' was in the Tower, having married without permission one of Her Majesty's maids of honour. This was, of course, Sir Walter Raleigh, explorer, poet, courtier, pirate and disgraced favourite of the Queen. Gingerly, Burghley mentioned his name to Elizabeth, but she had already reached the same conclusion, and the miscreant was temporarily released from prison.

Raleigh went straight to Dartmouth, where the weatherbeaten sea dogs greeted him with shouts of delight. In his official capacity as Lord Warden of the Stanneries

111

and Admiral of the West he had won friends throughout South Devon, his childhood home. Everybody from that part of the county followed his progress at Court, his romance with Bess Throckmorton and his imprisonment. And now the wayward Devon sailors, in a roundabout way, had engineered his release. A number of them knew him personally, having served under him on pirate voyages. Others had been part of the crew of the *Roebuck*, Raleigh's own ship, which had played a prominent part in the capture of the *Madre de Dios*.

Raleigh's knowledge of the men, his immense charisma, added to the fact that he spoke English with a broad Devonshire accent, assured him of success. Although he told the sailors 'I am still the Queen of England's poor captive', they were aware that if he performed his task to Elizabeth's satisfaction, he would probably soon be set free altogether. They also understood that much of the treasure in their own pockets was rightfully his, as a principal investor in the privateering venture. So they went along with him, while he turned a blind eye here and there, then had the *Madre de Dios* towed up the Channel and into the Thames, where the Council could impound her. The dealers and middlemen he sent packing. He spent several days carefully itemizing the cargo that remained, perhaps less than half the galleon's original contents. When he had finished, he returned to his prison.

When accounts for the undertaking were finalized, the Queen received a profit of about £75,000 and Raleigh £2,000; it should really have been the other way around, for Raleigh's investment in the venture far exceeded that of his monarch.

The *Madre de Dios* affair ended happily on the whole. Hundreds of Devon mariners who had risked their lives in capturing the treasure-ship were the main beneficiaries. Sir Walter endured two more months in the Tower before being granted his freedom, just in time to spend Christmas 1592 at Sherborne with his young bride.

A
Devonshire
Family

THIS is not, as you might imagine, a chronicle of one of Devon's illustrious families. It has nothing to do with the Courtenays, the Raleighs, the Drakes or the Rolles. This Devon family came from the opposite end of the social scale — in fact so far down it that they were nicknamed the 'North Devon Savages' or 'Naked People'! They were the Cheritons of Nymet Rowland.

They lived towards the end of the 19th century in a tumbledown cottage close to the ivy-covered, gloomy parish church of St Bartholomew. Nymet Rowland village, nestling in the Taw valley nine miles from Crediton, had a population of just under 100 in the days when the lawless behaviour of the Cheriton gang terrorized its inhabitants. In former times, the Cheritons had been decent yeoman farmers with 40 acres of freehold land growing wheat, barley and oats, but a succession of misfortunes and financial setbacks had reduced the family to a state of near destitution. Its members consisted of Christopher and his wife, three daughters, Eliza, Matilda and Charlotte, and the heir to the 'property', the only son, William.

As conditions deteriorated on the land and in the crumbling dwelling, so did the family scruples. Food was scarce, clothing ragged — so the only solution was to pinch somebody else's. Other people's crops were pilfered, kitchen gardens raided and washing lines stripped of useful garments. So successful were these nocturnal sorties that, far from appearing stunted or undernourished, the young Cheritons became renowned for their overpowering physical presence. Willie developed into a veritable giant, while the girls grew strong and lusty with unusually deep throaty voices.

In the course of time there were more occupants in the hovel — a girl and four boys — all grandchildren to Christopher. The fathers of these assorted illegitimate offspring chose to remain anonymous, so frightful rumours of incestuous goings-on began to circulate in the parish. Extra mouths to feed meant an ever-increasing dependence on the unwilling generosity of the villagers. However, the thieves did not go entirely unpunished. They were convicted on at least 50 occasions for petty offences ranging from extortion (half-a-crown!) to stealing vegetables.

As the years passed, the overcrowded cottage, more dilapidated than seemed possible, no longer had windows or doors — just gaping holes stuffed with straw. Beds, chairs, tables had long since fallen to bits and been burnt for fuel. The whole tribe slept in a pit dug in the floor, filled with filthy straw, into which they burrowed at night, huddled together for warmth.

During the summer months the girls scandalized passers-by because of the very scanty clothing which they wore while working in their semi-barren fields. But at least some of the young bloods of the area found the remarkable display of femininity too tantalizing to resist. Indeed, who could blame them? Three statuesque, sun-tanned wenches, overflowing with vitality and with unkempt tresses cascading down their backs? A nearby haystack with a hollowed-out 'room' provided a comfortable trysting-place for favoured admirers. Would-be lovers who did not come up to scratch were dispatched with a fearful volley of obscenities followed by stones and other missiles. The brood of young Cheritons mimicked the disgraceful behaviour of their mothers — shrieking curses at bystanders and pelting them with whatever came to grubby little fists. Even the Cheriton animals seemed adversely affected — the family bull, a monstrous creature, bellowed and roared in his field, frightening all within earshot.

And what of Willie? Huge, hairy, virile and violent, he was the brain behind most of the tribe's wrongdoings. Anyone foolhardy enough to stand in his way regretted it. One brave soul who tried it underwent the terrifying experience of being chased for more than a mile by a maddened Willie brandishing a fearsome axe. Another victim was the rector, Watkin Temple. Tired of the taunts of 'fat-gutted old passon' hurled at him when he rode by, he offered a gentle admonition. It brought forth dire consequences. The very next morning found him staring disconsolately at his ruined tennis lawn — wrecked by the four hefty Cheriton horses eating the lush grass and churning the remains into a muddy field. Nor was that the end of his punishment. Riding home alone at night past the Cheriton property, he was startled by a shadowy figure bolting into a hedge a little in front of him. Apprehensively he dismounted and, leading his horse, slowly proceeded along the road. He was soon halted by a stout barred gate lying across his path — a deadly obstruction for horse and rider. Willie's revenge for such a tiny check to his behaviour was savage indeed.

News of the barbarians eventually filtered through to London. A Fleet Street journalist, James Greenwood of the *Daily Telegraph*, decided to take a look at them. His journey began at Waterloo station and ended a few hours later with a one mile cross-country walk to Nymet Rowland from the station at Lapford. He located the disintegrating home of the Cheritons without difficulty and gained entry to it by the simple expedient of banging on the gate and asking for a drink of water from a female 'with a face tolerably clean,

115

and a pair of cheeks rosy as any Devonshire milkmaid's; a devil of a face all the same, with high cheek bones and a retreating forehead, and eyes deeply set in their orbits'. Since she did not reply, he summoned up his courage and entered the hovel. His first impression, of general filth and decay, was reinforced by the 'strong odour of pigs and their favourite food'. He counted seven human beings, plus miscellaneous livestock, but saw not one article of furniture in the place. He was rather disconcerted by the politeness of the female, who offered him a little jug of milk for his refreshment.

Greenwood's article, published on 23rd October 1871, described the Cheriton family somewhat unfairly, considering his own treatment, as 'bestial, filthy, and unexpressibly vicious'. He it was who first coined the name 'North Devon Savages' — an insult which, years later, was still applied to naughty North Devon children. His research uncovered another Cheriton living at Tedburn St Mary, south of Crediton. This was Elias, brother to Christopher. An eccentric character, he had made his home in a cask furnished with straw and rags 'just like a makeshift mastiff kennel' which he stuck under the hedge surrounding his land. Elias maintained that his tub was an extremely convenient abode because it could be turned around according to the direction of the prevailing wind. This harmless but bizarre conduct, coupled with the doings of the rest of the tribe, drove the journalist into a frenzy of Victorian rectitude. He could not believe that the Devon authorities had made no effort to 'wipe the disgrace from their county', and anticipated the happy day when 'the barbarians had been brought to acknowledge the iniquity of their ways'.

However, while Greenwood thundered about the lack of official action in dealing with the 'Savages', conditions in the Cheriton homestead had degenerated to such an extent that its previously robust occupants began to succumb to illness. Eliza, aged 31, perished from pneumonia in 1875. Christopher's youngest grandson also sickened and died. The rest of the family were stricken with an infectious disease in 1879 and were forcibly removed from their home to hospital. Although they eventually recovered, their absence from the village gave the inhabitants the chance to demolish the hovel. This caused the complete break-up of the Cheriton household, and its members dispersed, some emigrating. One of the boys made good by moving to London and becoming a policeman! Poor old Christopher, now in his seventies, was reduced to the life of a wandering beggar, but at length found sanctuary on his son-in-law's farm six miles away at Sandford Ash. Following Elias's example he slept in a cider barrel in an outhouse. In 1884 he accidentally set fire to his bedding and incinerated himself.

By 1889, Nymet House, described as a 'handsome modern house' with 'attached pleasure grounds' had been built on the site of Christopher's cottage. It was the residence of a respectable gentleman, Edgar Septimus Counsell Esq. The 'Naked People' were no more.

The Cruel Coast

FOR more than a week, the gailant old warship HMS *Ramillies* fought a tremendous battle. This was not against hostile ships from some foreign land — in defying such as these she had proved her worth time and time again — but a much more implacable foe, the forces of Nature. A combination of hurricane force winds, impenetrable fog and mountainous waves sought to drive her onto the vicious rocks of a cruel stretch of Devonshire coast which had witnessed many harrowing scenes, a graveyard of ships, where hundreds of vessels met their end.

The conflict began soon after the *Ramillies* left Plymouth on 6th February 1760 in convoy with six sister ships, bound for the Channel Fleet. Fierce southwesterlies knocked them off course and whirling sleet severely cut visibility. The tempest raged for a week, gradually becoming worse. Three of the ships were propelled down past Penzance; another eventually reached Portland, and another Spithead. The smallest, the cutter *Hawke*, was blown out into the middle of the Channel, where she sank with all her crew. The *Ramillies* acquitted herself bravely, riding the storm some dozen miles off the South Devon coast, but her great age at last told against her, and several alarming leaks began to appear, so that by 14th February, when the winds had reached their maximum force, she was compelled to seek the shore.

She had been pushed further east than anybody

realized, and when in appalling conditions the coastline dimly materialized, the sailing-master mistook Burgh Island, in Bigbury Bay, for Looe Island, west of Plymouth. The captain accordingly gave orders to steer east, but within minutes it became plain they were not running for Rame Head, outside Plymouth, but craggy Bolt Tail, the eastern extremity of Bigbury Bay. A desperate effort was made to bear off the land. They crowded on all the canvas they could, but in such ferocious winds this proved disastrous. The mainsail could not take the strain and split down the middle; the entire mainmast collapsed, then the mizzenmast crashed overboard. The captain immediately had the foremast and bowsprit felled and anchors cast. In the nick of time the great ship shuddered to a standstill 80 yards short of the black and glistening rocks. She held her position during the afternoon of 15th February, yet was so shrouded in fog that nobody on shore could see her, nor hear anything above the roaring gale.

As darkness fell, the remorseless battering of wind and water took its toll; one of the cables snapped, and the second instantly followed. Massive breakers now forced the *Ramillies* violently shorewards to the base of the sheer cliffs of Bolt Tail, where she smashed to pieces like a child's toy. Just before the fatal impact, a sailor who had taken his young lad to sea tried to throw the boy to safety, only to watch him dashed lifeless on the boulders. As the ship broke up, the sea swirled across the decks, sweeping everyone overboard.

Seven hundred people lost their lives on that dreadful night, and just 20 survived it. On the following morning Bigbury Bay presented the most horrifying scene, the water crowded with corpses and wreckage. Most of the ship's stern had been wedged into the rocks of an inlet, just east of Bolt Tail, which was thereafter known as Ramillies Cove. A surprisingly large number of the cannons were soon recovered, but little else. In 1906 a diver retrieved various items believed to come from the *Ramillies* — a brass

120

wheel, a sword handle, bits of a musket and some ammunition — the few pathetic remnants from so momentous an event.

Twelve years after the loss of the *Ramillies* another catastrophe took place in Bigbury Bay, involving the *Chantiloupe*, homeward bound from the West Indies, and hundreds of local people — to their eternal discredit. This was one of the worst instances of wrecking in Devon's history and rather different to the traditional legends so often recounted. You may have heard of the so-called 'wrecking parsons', and the tale is told of a minister in this area who, while preaching his 'zarmount', learnt by signal from the back of the church that a ship had gone to pieces nearby. Still expounding his text, he descended from the pulpit, tore off his surplice, strode down the aisle and at the doorway exhorted his flock, 'There's a wreck on the shore. Let's all start fair!' He then sprinted across the churchyard with the congregation in hot pursuit.

The incidents following the wreck of the *Chantiloupe* were far grimmer than this, as the local community swarmed along the beach fighting over rich cargo. The ship's only survivors were a seaman and a wealthy woman who staggered ashore utterly exhausted, shaking with cold and fright. Collapsing into the arms of those who waded out to meet her, she must have imagined her ordeal was over. But the worst was to come. These apparent rescuers stripped away her expensive clothes, removed her bracelets and necklaces, ripped out her earrings and, in their determination to miss nothing of the costly jewels, hacked off her ring fingers, after which they left her to perish on the sand. Somebody buried her there a little later, but her corpse was subsequently dug up by a dog. An examination suggested she was actually murdered. The unfortunate seaman may also have been killed, for in 1900 some children playing on the same part of the beach uncovered human bones and a skull.

The wreck of the *Jebba* at the foot of Bolt Tail in 1907

brought out a different side of the Devon character. Bound for Plymouth from Nigeria, the hapless steamer missed the Eddystone light through fog and came to grief in Bigbury Bay almost precisely where the *Ramillies* went to pieces. There were 155 on board, plus cargo worth £200,000. mostly fruit, palm oil and similar commodities. The ship's distress rockets were fired, alerting not only the Hope Cove lifeboat crew along the coast, but two fishermen, Isaac Jarvis and John Argeat, who immediately descended the precipitous 200 ft cliff in total darkness and rigged a boatswain's chair, taking off 117 people. The other passengers managed to escape by using various additional rescue equipment. Jarvis and Argeat also saved the ship's cat and two chimpanzees, who no doubt found the northerly latitudes in March quite enough of a new experience without being shipwrecked into the bargain. Several days later, bananas and pineapples were spotted floating past Lizard Point, 60 miles away.

Edward VII presented Isaac Jarvis and John Argeat with the Albert Medal for their valour. By a happy coincidence it now transpired that two of their great grandfathers had helped to rescue some of the pitifully few survivors from the *Ramillies* almost 150 years earlier.

The
Death Coach
of Lady Mary Howard

THE scene is Tavistock at the end of the 17th century. The time is midnight. The townsfolk are abed and the streets deserted. Nothing stirs. But . . . from the imposing gateway leading to Fitzford House a dark shape suddenly materialises — a huge black dog like a bloodhound, with glaring red eyes. He is followed by four sable horses drawing a coach made entirely of human bones. The coachman raising his whip to lash the horses into a gallop has no head. Inside the coach the pale figure of a woman can be vaguely discerned. The whole cavalcade races silently northwards, skirting Dartmoor's edge. Their goal is Okehampton Castle, 16 miles away. When they arrive, the hound plucks a single blade of grass from the castle mound and holds it carefully in his mouth. Soundlessly, dog, horses and coach swing round and hurtle back towards Tavistock. The hound places his blade of grass on a stone beside Fitzford Gate. As soon as his task is completed the ghostly procession vanishes. It will appear again on the next night, and the next, and on and on for hundreds of years, in a vain attempt to remove every blade of grass from the mound. The woman in the coach undergoing this endless penance is Lady Mary Howard.

She was born in 1596 at Fitzford House, the only child of

Bridget and John Fitz. Her father, just 21 at the time of her birth, had recently inherited the Fitzford estate as well as property in Cornwall and Kent. He had a large income at his disposal but, like many other young men, was quite unable to cope with the power it gave him. He changed rapidly from a sensible youth into a debauched and dissolute roué. As the infant Mary blossomed into girlhood, her father's headlong slide into degeneracy continued, causing him to be hated and feared by the people of Tavistock. He was known to have murdered at least two men — one of them his best friend, slain on Fitz's own doorstep outside Fitzford Gate. He finally lapsed into raving lunacy and committed suicide in a bloody fashion in August 1605.

The effect of this monstrous behaviour and its ghastly consequences on the nine year old Mary can hardly be imagined. But her troubles were not to end with the death of her father. She was now an heiress — a highly desirable commodity. Her wardship was quickly bought from King James I by the wily Earl of Northumberland. She cost him just £465 — a wonderful bargain. She was forcibly married off to the Earl's impecunious brother, Sir Alan Percy, when she was twelve and he 31. A marriage in name only, it nevertheless enabled Percy to get his hands on her fortune. Providentially for the reluctant bride, her husband caught his death of cold after a hunting expedition.

Mary, now 16, was already a beauty. She was spotted by the Earl of Suffolk, who felt she would be perfect for one of his sons. But the heiress was old enough to have romantic ideas of her own. She fell madly in love with a handsome youth of the same age — Thomas Darcy, son of Earl Rivers. They eloped before anyone was aware of their relationship, but her dreams of happiness were shattered when her bridegroom sickened and died within months of the wedding. Crushed by the tragedy, Mary allowed herself to be persuaded by the Earl of Suffolk to marry his fourth son, Sir Charles Howard. By him she had two daughters, Elizabeth and Mary. Sadly, the marriage was not a success. Sir Charles, continually in debt, paid his creditors by milking his wife's estates. Bitter animosity built up between them as Mary fought to regain some control of her property. Greatly resentful of her unwifely behaviour, Charles decided to leave her alone while he travelled in Europe. He returned to England in 1622, ready for another bout of matrimonial feuding, but Fate stepped in once more — he died unexpectedly in September of that year.

The rich and charming widow of 26 was a very different person from the twelve year old child bride pushed hither and thither by avaricious men. She was in control of her money and land and determined to remain so. She became an influential figure at the Court of Charles I's wife, Queen Henrietta Maria, renowned for her wit as well as her looks. The Duke of Buckingham was one of her favourites and he introduced her to his friend Sir Richard Grenville. This man became her fourth and last husband — the worst of the lot.

A son, Richard, was born to the couple at Fitzford House in 1630, but this happy event heralded the virtual end of her marriage. Mary had so tied up her estates that Grenville found it well-nigh impossible to get hold of any income. Furious arguments led to her being kept almost a prisoner in her own house. She escaped to sympathetic friends in London — in fact, to the home of her ex-brother-in-law Theophilus, now the second Earl of Suffolk, with whom she was on very good terms. With his help, she began proceedings to ensure that no money which was rightfully hers passed into Grenville's hands. The enraged husband hurled so much abuse at the Earl that the Star Chamber became involved in the row, its members deciding that a fine of £6,000 would be suitable compensation for the Earl's wounded pride. Of course, Grenville could not pay, so he spent the next three years languishing in the Fleet prison. During this time Mary petitioned for divorce, which was granted in 1632.

Grenville broke out of prison in 1633 and fled to Germany, where nothing was heard of him for seven years. His ex-wife, however, openly enjoyed her hard-won freedom. She discarded the hated Grenville name, calling herself Lady Howard for the rest of her life. She continued to live in London with the Earl of Suffolk, by whom she had a son, George. The Civil War was now raging, and in the general confusion she managed to conceal the facts of his parentage. But this same confusion allowed Grenville to slip back to England, where he joined the Royalist forces, gaining great favour with the King. He was installed at Fitzford House with a troop of cavalry on the King's orders, but when attacked by the Parliamentarians, retreated to Cornwall, leaving the house — Mary's house — to be wrecked and ransacked. From Cornwall he crossed the Channel, joining his son, Richard, in the Low Countries. He died at Ghent in about 1659. Of Richard the younger nothing more was heard.

Lady Mary, alone again apart from her beloved George since the death of the Earl of Suffolk, returned to Fitzford House and undertook extensive repairs to the war-damaged mansion. She hoped to live out her remaining years in peace, and for a little while this was so. But there was one great tragedy still in store for her. It occurred in September 1671, when George, a man in the prime of life, died suddenly. The shock was so dreadful that she followed him to the grave exactly one month later.

Not long after her death, exaggerated tales of her tempestuous career began to be told by the local people. It seems that, being the last member of the cursed Fitz family, Lady Mary was increasingly blamed for the wickedness perpetrated by her father in the town. Their two lives, in truth so different, became ever more entangled as gossip about the four husbands she had outlived grew more and more malicious. Memories of John Fitz's friend, murdered at Fitzford Gate, gave rise to claims of ghostly appearances at midnight, and thus the legend of the Death Coach of Lady Mary Howard was born. The woman whose life was one long battle against adversity was granted no peace in death.

Fitzford House has long since gone, although the haunted gateway still stands. Perhaps you might care to wait outside Fitzford Gate just before midnight? Remember, the first thing you will see is the huge dog with glaring red eyes. . . .

'My ladye hath a sable coach,
And horses two and four;
My ladye hath a black blood-hound
That runneth on before.
My ladye's coach hath nodding plumes,
The driver hath no head;
My ladye is an ashen white,
As one that long is dead.'